THE NEW COVENANT ROLE OF WOMEN IN LEADERSHIP

MARK DRAKE

The "SIMPLE BIBLE / SIMPLE GRACE / SIMPLE ANSWERS" Series
by MARK DRAKE.

TRUST DOESN'T COME FROM WHAT WE SAY ABOUT OURSELVES BUT WHAT TRUSTWORTHY PEOPLE SAY ABOUT US.

I consider Mark Drake to be finest teacher of New Covenant Grace alive today! I guarantee that it will be life changing! -**Larry Silverman- Pastor, Author**

You do not know me. I'm not anyone important. But none of that mattered to God. I received your book from my pastor and it changed my life.
—Donna- Alaska

Ordered your book. Read it! Loved it! Now, almost every page is underlined, starred, double starred, with comments, dog-eared pages, bracketed sections, and more comments. **—KB Tompkins- Alaska**

The New Testament Grace that Mark teaches is so easy to understand, practical, applicable and life changing...the hardest topics easy for the next generation and has translated his grace-base books into more than 10 languages, at his own cost, and then gives it all away.
—Sam Surendran, Penang

Mark Drake takes those often 'way-over-your-head' spiritual concepts and sets them in a tone of clarity, fascination, and freedom. His work, his writings, and his teachings have been groundbreaking, refreshing, and transforming.
-Steve Roberts, author, poet, designer, Malaysia

Mark Drake's teaching on grace has been transformational for our church. I strongly recommend his books and teaching material.
 -Steve Toliver- Pastor, Missionary

My biggest battles have not been persecution or intimidation, but fear, shame and condemnation. Mark's teaching helped changed all that.
-Underground Pastor in Middle East

I honestly do not know of anyone who has captured the true essence of the meaning of grace, as Mark Drake has.
-Micah Smith- Pastor, Author, International Missions Director

I hold to the statement of deep theological thought from the most high and holy reverend theologian, Dr. Seuss.

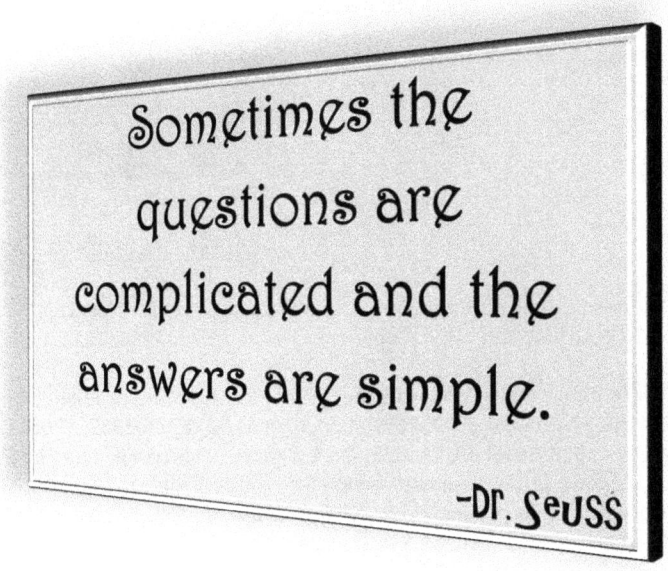

I will be grateful if you send me your questions or comments and help me grow in understanding.
askmark@markdrake.org

HELP! TYPOS- Each time I write a book, I do my best to have the manuscript proofread by many friends. But no matter how well we do, we seem to always miss some. When you find them, please send me an email so we can correct them in the next printing. I, and future readers, thank you!

Copyright © 2017 by MARK DRAKE
markdrake.org

Mark and Linda Drake

Unless otherwise noted, all Scriptural references are from the HOLY BIBLE, NEW INTERNATIONAL VERSION® NIV® Copyright © 1973, 1978, 1984, 2011 by Biblica, Inc.®

Other scripture quotations are either author's paraphrase or taken from the NEW AMERICAN STANDARD BIBLE (NAS), Copyright 1960, 1962, 1963, 1968, 1971, 1972, 1973, 1975, 1977, 1995, The Lockman Foundation. Used by permission, www.Lockman.org, King James Version (KJV) or Holy Bible, New Living Translation, copyright 1996, used by permission of Tyndale House Publishers, Inc., Wheaton, Illinois 60189. All rights reserved. THE MESSAGE: The Bible in Contemporary Language © 2002 by Eugene H. Peterson. All rights reserved.

All italics, bold print, underlining, and etc. are added by the author for emphasis and he takes responsibility for any inaccuracies in dates, places, or biblical interpretations.

Interior design work by Joe Geddes, Geddes Technology Consulting
Book cover designed by William Latocki ~ latocki.com

All rights reserved. No part of this book may be reproduced or transmitted in any form or by any means, electronic, mechanical, including photocopying, recording, or by any information storage and retrieval system, without written permission from the author.

ISBN 978-0-9843433-4-8

The "SIMPLE BIBLE / SIMPLE GRACE / SIMPLE ANSWERS" Series by Mark Drake.
This book focuses on one important topic and uses the topic to teach simple practices anyone can use to gain clearer Bible understanding on any subject.

For my daughters,
Lori Drake Jones
and
Amanda Drake Cromley,
and
my daughter-in-law,
Stacey Courtney Drake.

I am grateful that these strong women do not "hold back" from what God has created them to be and do. I am surrounded and supported by these courageous, confident women, and I am a better man because they fulfill their calling. And I thank God their daughters share the same strength of character!

MARK DRAKE- Anchorage, AK

THE NEW COVENANT ROLE OF WOMEN IN LEADERSHIP
Mark Drake

1) Major Mountain To Climb
2) Getting Ready To Rumble
3) The Reason For The Debate Is Real
4) Women In The Old Testament
5) The First Century Roman Empire
6) Jesus Changed Everything
7) Pentecost- Liberation Day For Women
8) Priscilla And Aquila Set The Model Of Pentecost
9) Paul's Apostolic "Fellow Workers"
10) Paul's Value For Women In Leadership
11) Phoebe, Romans, And Teaching Men
12) Did Paul Intend To Be Contradictory?
13) Cultural Norms, Localized Instructions And Eternal Truth
14) Temporary, Cultural Instructions For The Greater Good
15) The Challenge Of Our Own Bias
16) One Side Of The Conversation
17) What Did Paul Really Say About Women?
18) Usurping Authority, Eve's Sin, And Childbearing
19) The Culture Of Goddess Worship
20) Temporary Problem, Permanent Solution
21) Long Answers To Short Questions
22) Sincere, Important Questions

> The graphic layout of this book deliberately leaves space for you to make notes, write questions or scribble comments about the author. ☺

Chapter One

Major Mountain To Climb

We have a major, 2400 year old mountain we have to climb if we are going to think about women in leadership like the early apostles thought. If we don't think the way they thought, we will continue to disempower believing women; crippling over half of the Body of Christ. Throughout Church history, female believers have outnumbered male believers. Women have done most of the work, given most of the money, and served in nearly every capacity possible, except...leadership.

The challenge we face is how to remove the mountain of erroneous thinking that has been handed down to every generation of believers, from 300 BC to the 21st century. This erroneous thinking has crippled the Body of Christ and twisted the way we have viewed the Scripture for generations. And this mountain has been built by many of the world's *"greatest"* thinkers, philosophers, early *"Church Fathers,"* and *"Great Reformers."* For all the good these men have done, the damage to women, to the Church, to the world-wide Body of Christ, caused by the following statements, is nearly impossible to calculate.

I find the following beliefs so offensive that I originally left this chapter out as I wrote this manuscript. But the more I researched, and the more I understood how much damage these men have done, I felt I would be dishonest to the reader if I didn't include these painful statements. As a man, and a church leader, I am frankly embarrassed by what follows.

World Renowned Philosophers-

The courage of a man is shown in his ability to command. The courage of a woman is found in obeying. —Aristotle

By all means get married. If you get a good wife, you will be happy. If you get a bad wife, you will become a philosopher.
—Socrates

Women are those who fell prey to their irrational, emotional side, and are therefore incapable of reason and making rational choices...moreover as irrational beings, women may not always know what they really want and it is the man's domain to decide for them. —Plato

We have courtesans for our sex and pleasure. We have young slave prostitutes for our physical use and we have wives to bring up legitimate children. —Demosthenes

Do not admire your wife's beauty...from the time women are fourteen years old they think of nothing and aim at nothing except going to bed with men. —Epictetus

First Century Jewish Rabbinical Teaching-

Praise be to God that he has not created me a Gentile, a woman, or a hog. —First Century Jewish Prayer

Even the most virtuous of women is a witch.
—First Century Jewish Oral Law

The woman is inferior to the man in every way. —Josephus

If a man gives his daughter a knowledge of the Law, it is as though he taught her lechery. —bSot. 4.3

It is better that the words of the Law should be burned than that they should be given to a woman. —jSot. 3.4; 19a

Early Church *"Fathers"*-

Woman is a temple built over a sewer. It is contrary to the order of nature and of the law for women to speak in a gathering.
—Saint Jerome

Because of you we are punished by death...because of you, women, the Son of God had to die. —Tertullian

Men should not listen to a woman even if she says admirable things or if she says saintly things. They are of little consequence since they come from the mouth of a woman.
— Origen

A man may marry again if he has divorced his sinful wife because he is not restricted in his right as is the woman, because he is her head. —Ambrose

There is nothing for a man that is shameful, for a man is endowed with reason. But for women, it brings shame to even reflect on that she is. —Clement of Alexander

By herself woman is not the image of God. The man, on the other hand, alone, is the image of God. We should look upon the female state as if it were being a deformity. —Augustine

For a man to go to a woman for advice is like going to the lowest kind of animal to seek advice. —Chrysostom

Woman is defective and misbegotten...Woman is naturally subject to man because in man the discernment of wisdom predominates.
—Thomas Aquinas

The wickedness of women is greater than all other wickedness. A dragon is more curable than the familiarity of a woman. Avoid them like poisonous animals. —Pope Innocence III

The "*Reformers*"

There is no gown or garment that worse becomes a woman than when she would be wise. —Martin Luther

Let the woman be satisfied with the state of her subjection and that she is made inferior to the more distinguished sex. Because she receives her origin from man she is therefore inferior in rank. All women are born that they may acknowledge themselves as inferior to the male. —John Calvin

To make women learned and to make a fox tame work out to the same end. Educating a woman or a fox simply makes them more cunning. —King James

After copying these statements from their historical sources, I wish I could apologize on behalf of all men. But, these are the beliefs that have influenced the way the Bible passages about women have traditionally been understood. And, since we are on a search for truth and not just personal opinion, let's climb this mountain and wade into the fight.

"Church, we have a problem; a real problem!"

Chapter Two

Getting Ready To Rumble

"Wanna start a fight?" Just get a bunch of male church leaders together and suggest that we ought to put more women in leadership positions in our churches. Then step back and watch the "fun" begin! Few issues stir up angry debate among godly, loving Christians like the subject of women in ministry and leadership. Friends have separated, churches split, and entire denominations have divided over this issue. But, we are talking about the activity, function and destiny of approximately <u>60% of all believers</u>; women. If 60% of our physical body was severely affected, we would certainly want to get the treatment correct!

> **I understand this is a very important subject. A sincere but incomplete reading of Scripture, with no understanding of first century culture, will leave anyone confused.**

I Want To Be Very Clear At The Start-

I want to assure you; by the time you get to the end of this book some complicated things will become simple. You may not agree with all I have written, but my reasoning and my sources will be simple to understand and easy to confirm.

I am not asking you to take my word for what I am presenting as *"truth."* And you should not *"just take my word for it,"* or anyone else's. Everything must be examined and proven. The resources listed in the

back are easily accessed by anyone and they clearly validate everything I have come to believe. I may not interpret them all perfectly but the historical facts are the facts.

My strong belief is that this subject is much too important to not get it right and I do believe accuracy in God's Word is essential. I do understand this is a difficult subject because some verses <u>seem</u> to clearly contradict each other. A sincere but incomplete reading of Scripture can leave anyone very confused about God's position concerning women in leadership. As a result, the Church seems to be generally divided into two opposing positions.

> **We must not *"just take someone's word for it."* Not mine or anyone else.**

Generally speaking, the most "*liberal*" churches seem to have no problem ordaining women to do virtually anything because of their belief that the Bible is outdated. I am not endorsing this point of view. On the other end of the spectrum, some of the most strongly charismatic churches ordain women to lead in virtually any capacity because of the belief that the only thing that truly matters is the *"anointing."* I am also not endorsing this point of view.

Just mention the subject of women in leadership and you never know when a fight may break out. Anything from a war of words and name-calling about the "*spirit of Jezebel*" and women motivated by the devil to rule over wimpy, weak-kneed, cowardly men with no Holy Ghost backbone, to accusations of chauvinistic, misogynistic, caveman-minded men who just want to keep "*their*" women in the kitchen or doing laundry, but definitely not leading. On the other extreme, there are those churches who believe the Bible is simply a book of general guidelines and much too outdated to be literally applied today.

Some churches seem to just ignore the verses that appear to disagree with their view. On the other hand, some churches attempt to dance around verses that seem to contradict their particular point of view with practices that actually appear to border on the bizarre.

Some churches ordain women and simply say, *"We feel the anointing on them so obviously we are right."* Some other churches take the position that *"the Bible is outdated when it comes to women's rights and we are bringing the Church out of the dark ages into the 21st century."*

Some churches will allow a woman to teach, but only if her husband stands beside her to *"cover"* her as she speaks. This is apparently so the devil can't spread deception through her because women are *supposedly* more easily deceived than men. Or, a woman can speak if she stands down on the main floor and not up on the stage behind the pulpit. Some say this is permissible because speaking from the main floor is not actually preaching or teaching, but simply *"sharing"*; using an outline, dozens of Scripture passages and illustrations...for an hour...but still just *"sharing"*. However, standing on the stage behind the pulpit is preaching or teaching and Paul supposedly forbids this practice.

I'm not making this up, although I wish I were.

GOOD STORIES
OR
GOOD SCRIPTURE
OR BOTH

As we tackle this serious subject we have to decide if we are going to build our foundation on good stories, good Scripture, or both.

Anecdotes, Anointing and Original Languages-

There are many excellent writings by highly educated scholars on this very controversial subject. Having read many of them, I am attempting to approach this subject using the simple methods I believe we should use when seeking to understand any seemingly *"difficult"* passage or topic in Scripture.

-Anecdotal/Anointing Evidence-

Some writers base their primary argument on the many wonderful stories and anecdotes of how God has, and is, using women to extend the Kingdom. The thinking goes something like this-

"God uses this woman so powerfully. Her method, message, and character must be right or God wouldn't use her like that."

"Look at the fruit of her anointing! She must be doing the right thing."

I think in the heart of every believer, regardless of the position we take on women in ministry, we all rejoice when the Gospel is declared and the Kingdom grows. Even if for some, the rejoicing is done privately and very quietly because of the opposing views of others around them.

Possible Danger Ahead-

My concern with basing our *"proof"* on anecdotal or *"anointing"* evidence is that God has always used imperfect *"earthen vessels"* for Kingdom purposes. But that doesn't mean He put His approval on all the methods used or the character of the *"vessel"* being used. *(Balaam, Sampson,*

> "God uses this woman so powerfully. Her method, message, and character must be right or God wouldn't use her like that."
> "Look at the fruit of her anointing! She must be doing the right thing."

Moses, and I all come to mind here.) Just because God blesses a person and their method, does not mean it's the most appropriate or most godly method or message. It does mean that God is a very good God to use people like us, in spite of ourselves!

"But this happened in the Bible...once."

Another potential problem in using anecdotal evidence to establish doctrine and practice is there are many things in the Bible which God did only once. Though we know He can do whatever He chooses, however and whenever He chooses, we must not make these one-time happenings our doctrine and normal practice. Although, I wish things like teleportation were normal because it would make it easier on me.

Philip was apparently instantly transported from one place to another, many miles away (Acts 8:39). But it only happened once as far as we are told. With all the planes I fly on, I would love it if teleportation was the normal church practice, or at least, the tenth gift of the Spirit.

On the other hand, Jesus spit, made mud to put on a man's eyes, and healed his blindness...once. I am glad we don't teach the *"divine mud method"* as the standard practice for ministering to the blind. I know God sometimes gives miracle babies but I don't think many of us want to make the Abraham/Sarah miracle our doctrine and normal practice, or we will have lots of 100 year old new fathers and mothers out there!

Original Languages And How Definitions Have Changed-

Other writers go deep into original languages and present very scholarly, academic reasons for their position about women in leadership, and I have benefitted greatly from their efforts. However, these books are often very difficult for the average Christian to understand. And for those who know nothing about original languages, arguments over what appear to be *"jots and tittles"* may seem like little more than sleight-of-hand and a bit suspicious, simply because they are complicated for us.

However, the *"original languages"* were not complicated for the people to whom the New Testament letters were written. First century Greek was the same to Paul's audience as 21st century English is to mine. Fortunately, there are many trustworthy scholars who have done much of the original language work for us in our various Bible translations and many study aids. We are happy to recommend the ones we have found to be trustworthy listed in the back for your more in-depth study.

The primary challenge we have today is making sure that we are defining words the same way the writers defined them. Definition will become a major theme in other parts of this series. All communication depends on common definition.

> *All communication depends on common definition.*

Is *"coke"* a drink or a narcotic? Is *"boot"* footwear or the trunk of a car? Is *"sharp"* the condition of a knife or a kind of cheese?" *"Air"* in English is what we breathe. But in Indonesia, *"air"* means water. Real communication is impossible without clear definitions. However, agreeing on a common definition so we can understand each other doesn't have to be difficult. It simply requires a few logical questions.

-Simple Gospel And The Inability To Read-

The overwhelming majority of people in the first century could not read. Most studies say only 3-5% of the Roman Empire were truly literate and that was mainly among the wealthy, civic leaders and scribes. Of course, this varied some from nation to nation and the numbers may have been a bit higher in Jerusalem because most boys were taught to read the Torah. (*However, females were never allowed to be taught*.)

Imagine the difficulty the apostles had as they wrote instructional teaching letters to the churches throughout the Empire. These letters contained the most important truths in the world. They had to send those letters with couriers who would be able both to read them and give explanation to the questions that would surely and constantly arise.

This is why men like Paul, though brilliant, wrote in the simplest terms possible. Simple to the people he wrote to, in the context of the time and culture in which they lived. We must not forget this. In fact, Paul warned his readers to not move away from the simplicity in Christ.

> **OVER 95% OF PEOPLE IN THE FIRST CENTURY COULD NOT READ AND YET GOD HAS PRESERVED HIS WORD OF TRUTH BY HIS SPIRIT OF TRUTH!**

> "But I am afraid that, as the serpent deceived Eve by his craftiness, your minds will be led astray from the **simplicity** and purity of devotion to Christ." (2 Cor. 11:3 NASB)

This is why I've spent years reading the Bible and looking for the most simple, logical explanations. I believe that's how God inspired the written Word to be understood. I also appreciate the importance and difficulty of translating from ancient languages into modern speech; both the good and bad of these important efforts. Of course, God knew all of this ahead of time because He is the One who created the first differences in language. He has faithfully protected His truth throughout the centuries, and the increase of languages, by His Spirit of Truth.

I have attempted to use a mixture of the above methods in my research, and present my findings in a simple, logical way. I have become completely convinced that God's intention has always been for His Word to be simple, logical, and clear for all who will follow simple, basic rules of understanding.

> **God is the One who created different languages and He planned for all the challenges. He has faithfully protected His truth by His Spirit of Truth, even as languages have changed throughout the centuries.**

Chapter Three

The Reason For The Debate is Real

Unbelieving critics of the Scripture have always sought to prove that the Bible is seriously inaccurate and highly contradictory, therefore, untrustworthy. We believers have always sought to prove the reliability of the Scripture by showing that, when read like any other literature that is a combination of dozens of writers over a period of thousands of years, the Bible is indeed divinely-inspired and not simply of human origin.

However, in order to stay true to the accepted rules of interpreting and understanding any literature, we have to deal with the seemingly contradictory passages with truthfulness and honesty. And we do have some verses that certainly seem to create a conundrum for sincere seekers and the reason for this *"women in ministry"* debate is real.

-Was Paul Confusing To The Corinthian Believers?

I have often wished that Paul would have thought about the confusion he was going to cause 2000 years later when he wrote some of his instructions about women's roles in the church. Of course, Paul couldn't have done that because he wasn't thinking about us and he couldn't have factored in our cultural views.

> PAUL WASN'T THINKING ABOUT 21ST CENTURY READERS

He was writing to a specific group of people, in a specific geographical area, in a specific period of time, facing a specific set of problems. One thing we can be sure of; his readers weren't confused. They understood the cultural issues of their day and he was writing TO them, not TO us, 2000 years later. Thankfully, God knew exactly what He was doing, then and now. The more I can *"put myself in the place of a first century reader,"* the better chance I have of truly understanding what was written TO them, and how to apply it FOR me today.

So my opinion of how Paul *"should"* have worded his letters is worthless because he was writing to them, not to me. We will be digging into verified cultural issues of the first century to increase our understanding of what Paul was writing about. But here is a simple, though important mistake we frequently make in the way we often read the Bible today.

-Never Read Just "A" Bible Passage-

As I travel around the world training young leaders who are influencing huge parts of the world-wide Body of Christ, it's fairly easy to see why so many people view the Bible as complicated and hard to understand. What makes this so sad is that we seem to understand how to interpret other written material but many think the process changes when we read the Bible. Though there are several fundamental processes we must use in understanding any literature, one of the simplest, yet most often violated is…

> **Never read just "a" Bible passage to decide what the writer meant.**

Never read just "a" Bible passage to decide what the writer meant.

Common sense readers would never read just one line out of the middle of Shakespeare and assume they knew what Sir William intended. We would never read a paragraph from the middle of the Declaration of Independence and seriously think we now understood what our founding fathers meant. Or read one part of our US Constitution and believe we could now understand how to make a democracy work.

And why not? Because things written in one part of a document help explain things written in other parts. One right in our nation's brilliant Bill of Rights is limited or further defined by other rights. And it's only when we understand the importance of *"context and culture"* and *"comparing all the passages that refer to the same subject,"* do we begin to understand the original intent of the authors and what it meant to the audience to whom they were writing.

Once again, the more I can *"put myself in the place of a first century reader,"* the better chance I have of truly understanding what was written TO them, and how to apply it FOR me today.

> **How would a first century believer read these letters?**

So Let's Look At Some Of These *Admittedly Difficult* Passages.
(All emphasis and underlining in the following verses are mine)

> *"A woman should learn in quietness and full submission. I do not permit a woman to teach or to have authority over a man; she must be silent."* (1 Tim. 2:11-12)

> *"...women should remain silent in the churches. They are not allowed to speak, but must be in submission, as the Law says. If they want to inquire about something, they should ask their own husbands at home; for it is disgraceful for a woman to speak in the church."* (1 Cor. 14:34-35)

If we stop here, the issue *seems* clear and the solution *seems* easy.

1) **Men** are to preach, teach and lead in everything.
Simple...Clear...Easy to follow.

2) **Women** are to stay silent in church.
Simple...Clear...Easy to follow.

It does seem very simple, clear and easy to follow...until we read other seemingly contradictory verses in the same epistles; some even in the very same chapter! Verses that seem to say exactly the opposite!

Then it's not so simple...or clear...or easy to follow!

If we back up three chapters we read this- "...every <u>woman who prays or prophesies (in the church)</u>..." (1 Cor. 11:5)

Simple logic would ask, *"How can women pray or prophesy in church but <u>keep silent at the same time?"</u>*

> Contradictory verses in the same epistles, in the same chapter? Verses that seem to say exactly the opposite? So it's not simple, or clear, or easy to follow?
> <u>Or, is it?</u>

It certainly *seems* that we are given directly contradicting instructions by the same author, in the same letter, in the same chapter about a woman's function in church meetings. Let's do a simple exercise of logic with one main *"conflicting"* passage.

> *"<u>When you come together</u>, <u>everyone</u> has a hymn, or a word of instruction, a revelation, a tongue or an interpretation. <u>All of these must be done</u> for the strengthening of the church."*
> (1 Cor. 14:26)

Asking Logical Questions

Let's walk through this verse and ask some logical questions. This alone, will not solve our problem, but it may show us there is more to this story than a quick reading might indicate. If we see there is more to the story than we can find in just a couple of verses, then we can start asking logical questions. And that puts us on our way to understanding what Paul meant since we know he didn't intend to be confusing. Although, we will probably get a bit more confused before we begin to gain more understanding.

-*"When you come together..."*
-Does this seem to be a church gathering of both men and women?
-*"Everyone has..."*
-Did Paul believe the word *"everyone"* meant just men?
-*"All of these must be done..."* -Does this sound like Paul intended for just men to participate in *"these things"*?

-Can **everyone** contribute to the meeting in these vocal gifts, if over half the attendees (women) must remain *silent*?

In just five verses later we read this-
> *"For you can **all prophesy** in turn so that **everyone may be instructed** and encouraged."* (1 Cor. 14:31)

-Again, did Paul believe the word *"all"* referred to only men?
-Did Paul believe that a woman can prophesy while staying *silent*?
-If prophesying will cause *"everyone to be **instructed**,"* and *"everyone"* must include men, then are women supposed to instruct men through prophecy, but *"not teach men"* and still *"remain silent"*?

Let's put all these verses together and add the confusion at the end-

"Ladies, since you are included in 'everyone', when the church meets, you should feel free to lead out in prayer, prophesy, sing a hymn, give instruction or a revelation, a tongue or interpretation. HOWEVER, you must remain silent while doing so."
(1 Cor.11:5, 14:26, 31, 34-35, 1 Tim. 2:11-12)

Huh?!?! I thought this was supposed to be simple?!?!

With these apparent contradictions in the same epistle, and even in the same chapter, I understand why people have such differing beliefs and why they hold to them so strongly. And yet, the answer still seems to be the same-

>...consider context,
>...comprehend culture,
>...compare Scripture with all Scripture on the same topic.

Remember, although we are dealing with the specific topic of women in church leadership, the principles we are going to apply should be used in all Bible study. Especially when we are dealing with verses that seem to directly contradict other verses.

They Understood Him-

> **Consider Context, Comprehend Culture, Compare Scripture With Scripture.**

Of course, we must never forget that Paul's readers understood what he was writing about. One thing we can be sure of, though we may be confused, they were not. They understood the immediate problems that caused Paul's response and the cultural issues they faced every day. Instructions like these were not considered difficult or confusing, but simple guidance from their spiritual father.

The confusion we face comes from not reading the Scripture the way they did. If I put myself in the mindset of a first century believer, instead of a 21st century believer, then I would have a much better chance of understanding the cultural differences and the problems they faced then. When I do that, I can read these letters, not as complicated, deeply mysterious oracles, but as helpful instruction from a loving spiritual father. I would read it expecting it to be simple to understand.

Understanding their pagan background and the *"religious culture"* they were delivered out of, yet lived in the midst of, it makes sense that Paul would take extra care to be simple and clear.

Since Paul was a leading expert on the Old Testament, and the Corinthian believers had very little exposure to the Old Testament, could Paul's instructions be based on his in-depth understanding of God's original intention for men and women?

Perhaps Paul really did understand God's eternal intention for women by understanding the *"shadow"* of how He used them in clear, important leadership capacities in the Old Testament. Perhaps Paul understood that the best model to follow is God's.

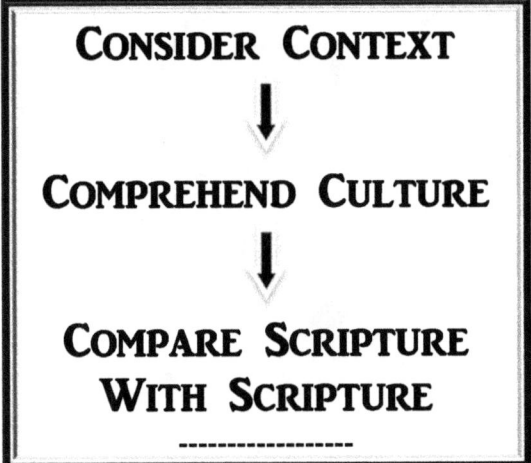

Chapter Four

Women In The Old Testament

The Bible tells us the truth about what people did both good and bad, and how God has always worked within the limitations of fallen human nature. This means that the events recorded are true in that they happened, but they were certainly not always right. Slavery, polygamy, divorce, wars, and many other things were done in different cultures and different situations. Although God worked within these behaviors to reach the hearts of people, He did not declare them eternally right or just. These terrible things were the result of fallen, corrupt human nature and certainly not what a good and just God desires for His creation. But a good and just God also gives His creation the ability to choose their own future, even though their choices often go against what He desires for them.

As Jesus said about divorce, *"...it is not what God originally intended."*
(Matt. 19:8 NLT)

Even though so many of the events recorded were the result of the choices of fallen nature and *"not what God originally intended,"* God's great love is shown in the way He made provision for the failures of people and didn't just cut them off for being so imperfect. In every case, God offered redemption for those who would choose it.

The Bible also contains several instructions about women, marriage, divorce, and widowhood that, though they seem strange to our culture, were actually meant for the protection of women in difficult situations and in vastly different cultures. There was no *"safety net"* in these ancient cultures, no divorce courts, Social Security or welfare. And because women were considered property, widows and divorced women especially were at the mercy of any man who wanted to take advantage of them. Laws concerning things such as *"bride price,"* *"redeemer kinsman,"* and many others that seem so strange to us today were actually good commandments given so widows and abandoned women would be taken care of within Jewish culture.

Differences In Old Testament And New Testament Judaism-

As we will see in a coming chapter, the extremely chauvinistic view of women practiced in first century Judaism did not come from the Law or Old Testament instruction. The Jewish leaders in Jesus' day were terrified that the Jewish people would lose their national identity due to the influence of the surrounding Greek/Hellenistic culture. They responded by grossly twisting Old Testament teaching and adding hundreds of man-made rules based on their sexist beliefs that women were the cause of all sexual sin and had little value above cattle.

> *"...it is not what God originally intended."*
> **(Matt 19:8 NLT)**

God Empowers Whom He Will-

Clearly, since it was God who empowered people to do His will in the Old Testament, God has always seen women capable of anything He wanted them to do. The Old Testament has an abundance of passages that show God chose to use many women in very significant leadership ways throughout Israel's history. The stories of women such as Sarah, Rahab,

Miriam, Ruth, Esther, Deborah, and many others, are celebrated by both Christians and Jews.

The Old Testament passages which tell the many stories of how God used women, sometimes to save the entire nation of Israel, are instructive to read. But since we are focusing on the role of women in the New Covenant we will not examine them here.

Perhaps He Couldn't Find a Few Good Men-

However, some people maintain that God didn't WANT to use women in the Old Testament because they are so inferior to men they are unsuited for any leadership role. But, when confronted with the many Old Testament examples where He did use women in the highest leadership roles, some maintain He **_had_** to use a woman because He couldn't find a man who would obey Him at the time.

If the superiority and *"covering"* of men were so important to God, do we really believe the Holy Spirit could not empower at least ONE man to obey Him in any of these critical Old Testament situations? God anointed several men who had serious character failures when there was an important job that needed to be done. *(Insert men like Samson here.)* He didn't seem to have a problem using anyone if He chose to. He never seemed to run short of angels to do His bidding, either.

Is the God who simply spoke, and the worlds leapt into existence, ever so far out of options that He must violate (as some suggest) His own *"eternal principle"* to get something done?

God opened the mouth of a donkey to speak His Word on one occasion. On another, He forced a false prophet to speak His truth, even though he was under the threat of death by the king who hired him. So it's a bit difficult to believe God used these women throughout the Old Testament because it was the ONLY option He had.

> **IS GOD EVER SO FAR OUT OF OPTIONS THAT HE MUST VIOLATE (AS SOME SUGGEST) HIS OWN "ETERNAL PRINCIPLE" TO GET SOMETHING DONE?**

(The following cultural facts about conditions in the first century Roman Empire are documented in the materials referenced in the back of this book.)

Chapter Five

The First Century Roman Empire

When reading about the founding of the United States, it's easy to see how our language and customs have radically changed. From allegiance to England, to slavery, to the slaughter of my forefathers, (native Americans) to the prohibition of women to have equal rights with men; things have changed greatly over the past 200-300 years. And as we read historical writings from the 1600-1800s, we take into account the cultural differences that have occurred over the past 200-300 years. If we didn't, it would be impossible to understand many of the cultural differences that led our founding fathers to make some of the choices they made.

If we didn't factor in the many changes made over the past 200 years, we wouldn't even be able to understand much of writing of that era because so many words have changed in so many ways. And that's just looking at the past 200 years. But what about the changes over the past **two thousand years**?

> If I don't factor in the cultural and language changes that have taken place over the past 2000 years, I'll never understand what the biblical writers intended.

Each time we read the New Testament, we must remind ourselves to put the language and customs into the context of the first century; not 200 years ago, but 2000 years ago. The vastness of the Roman Empire, the many countries Rome ruled over, and the huge differences in first century cultures, must also be factored into our understanding as we read the New Testament. It's not all that difficult; it just takes some simple reasoning and awareness. An important part of our awareness when we read a *"difficult"* passage is to regularly think, *"There must be more to this story."*

> When we read a *"difficult"* passage, we are wise to remind ourselves, *"There must be more to this story."*

There were many differences in the cultures, customs, and taboos within the many different countries that made up the first century Roman Empire. Roman Caesars tended to allow conquered areas to maintain their unique customs and religious beliefs unless they posed a clear and present danger to the Empire.

In Egypt, at the far end of the Empire, women were treated almost as equals. Marriages were often monogamous and commonly by mutual consent. Women frequently had equal rights in education and inheritance. Because of these rights, many women were able to become wealthy and through their wealth acquire political power. A few women even ruled as pharaohs. But this treatment of women was rare throughout the rest of the Empire where they were basically property.

It Was Truly A Man's World-

Most of the Roman Empire was firmly committed to patriarchy and the subordination of women. By the time Jesus came, most cultures had been influenced by men like Aristotle to believe that man was completely superior, woman was completely inferior. It was widely believed that husbands and fathers should rule over their wives and daughters in everything.

> These cultural facts are documented by the reference material in the back of this book.

Only men were thought capable of being educated, since women did not have the mental capacity for anything more than simple thought. This resulted in the vast majority of women being illiterate and strictly forbidden to be educated. Their role was limited to obedience and silence; children and home.

In most countries within the Empire, women were under the complete control of the male head of the extended family unit. Male authority ruled over nearly every area of life and death. In some places, a death penalty could be imposed upon a woman for adultery or drinking alcohol. The male head often arranged marriages and appointed guardians for the women of his family. In many countries, a woman could not legally transact business, make a contract or a will, testify in court, or free a slave without the approval of her guardian.

Polygamy was common in many places because women were considered objects of property. Paul's injunction to Timothy that *"elders and deacons must be husbands of one wife"* makes sense when applied to men. But this would never have been applied to women being considered for leadership because a woman could not have more than one husband. It would never have factored into the consideration.

Because the Roman Empire was so large, there were exceptions concerning the role of women from country to country in issues such as education and business, and we read about some of them in the New Testament. There are several references to women who financially supported the ministry of Jesus, and later, many of the apostles and local churches throughout Asian provinces. This demonstrates how God utilized the exceptions to advance the position of women in general society. There is overwhelming historical evidence to prove that wherever Christianity spread, the treatment of women became much more humane and *"equality"* grew.

First Century (Second Temple) Jewish Culture-

Scholarly theological writings frequently refer to the Jews of the first century as *"Second Temple Jews."* This differentiates the worship, customs and culture between the Temple built by Solomon in 957 BCE, destroyed by the Babylonians in 586 BCE, and the second Temple rebuilt under Ezra and Nehemiah in 515 BCE. This Second Temple went through various attempts at destruction by Jewish enemies but was renovated and expanded by Herod in 20 BCE, just a few years before Jesus was born into the world. This second expanded Temple is the one we read about in the New Testament which was totally destroyed by Roman armies in 70 AD just as Jesus prophesied in Matthew 24. The Temple has never been rebuilt.

This historical perspective about the *"Second Temple Jews"* is important for our study because during the first century, religious leaders fought hard against the Greek influence in *"Second Temple Judaism."* As a result, the rabbis dramatically increased the number of *"laws,"* became far more *"legalistic"* in the enforcement of these *"laws,"* and far stricter in trying to keep the people separate from Greek or Hellenistic influence. One of the ways they sought to be separate was a dramatic increase in the prohibitions placed on women.

Women were even more restricted in first century Judaism than they had been in the Old Testament. Being under the control of Rome caused the

Jewish leaders to impose even stronger restrictions on everyday life out of fear that Greek and Roman influence would degrade Jewish society even more.

In general, Jewish women were legally the property of men. Before marriage, a girl was the property of her father and could not choose who she would marry. After marriage, she became the property of her husband. In some cases, women could engage in certain kinds of business and widows could, in limited cases, inherit the family wealth when her husband died.

> **It Was Much Worse for Women in First Century Israel than in the Old Testament**

Second Temple Rabbinic Views Were Stridently Misogynistic-

Women were described not only as evil temptresses, but also as witches and nymphomaniacs. They were further caricatured as greedy, vain, lazy, and frivolous. Rabbinic society was for the most part monogamous, but polygamy was still permitted to rabbis.

Divorce was easy for a man to obtain but impossible for a woman. Divorce was compulsory if a wife was childless for ten years. A man could obtain a divorce simply if a woman went out without a veil, conversed in public with other men, or did not give complete, unquestioning, and immediate obedience to their husband.

This is the mentality that brought the challenge from the Pharisees, *"Can a man divorce his wife for **any** reason?"* (Matt.19:3)

First Century Jewish Women Could Never Be Teachers-

Jewish women were never allowed to speak in public since they were uneducated, couldn't read and were believed to be untrustworthy. Synagogue worship was segregated, with women never allowed to participate in any way. There was no opportunity for women to ever develop the ability to participate in discussions with educated men; certainly, never learn how to teach or simply speak in public. Most women couldn't even ask reasonable questions. Any attempt would look much like a kindergartener trying to ask a question in an advanced calculus college course. The very idea would be viewed, at the least, as a joke, and at the worst, a sacrilege!

Whatever the reasons for Paul's instruction that *"women are not to teach,"* they clearly had something to do with the cultural obstacles that would have to be overcome for most (though not all) women to develop even the most elementary ability to simply ask reasonable questions, long before they could be equipped to teach.

Jesus Came Into A Jewish Culture Where Most Women...
...were not allowed to recite the prayers at meals.
...could not testify in court since men taught that the genetic makeup of women made them untrustworthy.
...were barred from studying the writings of Moses (Torah), the most basic and bedrock words of God for the Jews.
...were not allowed to learn how to read.
...were not permitted to receive any education.
...were not allowed to even ask questions in public.

These were not laws or practices given by Moses. These things were added after Israel was conquered by Rome and the rabbis feared the Jews would be too influenced by Greek/Hellenistic culture. Sadly, they ended up treating women as bad as the surrounding pagan cultures.

> **Just imagine living where men were taught to give thanks to God each morning that they had not been created as a woman!**

Is This An Exaggerated View Of First Century Jewish Culture?

I read the Scripture with my own bias, as we all do. Our goal is to keep growing in our understanding so we read and understand the first century epistles the way a first century believer understood them.

But just in case someone think my personal views might cause me to over-state the radically degrading view of all women, read just a small sample of documented writings from the leading rabbinical teachers that shaped the thinking of Jews when Jesus came on the scene.

"Any iniquity is small compared to a woman's iniquity.... From a woman sin had its beginning, and because of her we all die"
(Sirach 25:19, 24; 2nd century B.C.).

"Better is the wickedness of a man than a woman who does good; it is woman who brings shame and disgrace" (Sirach 42:14)

"The woman is inferior to the man in every way"
(Josephus, Against Apion 2:201).

*"A man is required to say the following three blessings every day: 'Blessed are you who have not made me a heathen, **who have not made me a woman**, who has not made me ignorant."* (bMen. 43b; Ber. 7.18)

"There is no wisdom in woman except with the spindle" (bYom. 66b).

"It is better that the words of the Law should be burned than that they should be given to a woman" (jSot. 3.4; 19a).

"If a man gives his daughter a knowledge of the Law, it is as though he taught her lechery" (bSot. 4.3).

> *"Blessed are you...who have not made me a woman..."*

The Second Temple Was Designed To Keep Women Out-

Believing that God created females genetically inferior to males, Jewish leaders severely limited women's access to the most important thing in all Jewish worship; the very Temple itself! The architecture of the Second Temple, frequently called Herod's Temple, was deliberately designed to prohibit women from being involved in the most sacred elements of Jewish worship and national identity as the *"People of God."*

When a worshipper approached the Temple in the first century, the first area was the Court of the Gentiles. Converted Gentiles could go no further than this first area. Five steps above the Court of the Gentiles was the women's court. Jewish women could enter this area, but go no further.

> **The architecture of the Second Temple prohibited women from the most sacred elements of worship**

Fifteen steps *(15 STEPS!)* above the women's court was the Jewish men's court and access to the all the sanctified articles used for sacrifice and worship. Women were never allowed into this area for one basic reason, they were genetically female. The result was simple and sad. Men were given far more privileges to worship God than were women.

When Jesus came into the world, things began to rapidly change. The fulfillment of Pentecost demonstrated that God intended to fill and use

BOTH men and women equally, as His servants. And the early church quickly became a counter-culture to Jewish, Greek, and Roman culture.

Important Questions We Must Answer

-With this mountain of evidence about the extreme Jewish beliefs in the inferiority and degradation of women, is there any question that the apostles had an uphill battle in teaching most women and equipping them to one day teach others?

-How could believing women ever assist in fulfilling the Great Commission if they were not allowed to *"teach them what I have taught you"*? (Matt. 28:18)

-How could women fulfill the expectations given for every believer, such as *"...by this time you ought to be teachers..."*? (Heb. 5:12)

-How could women, in whom Christ lived, allow the Spirit to express Himself through them in church gatherings such as *"When you come together, everyone has a hymn, or a word of instruction, a revelation, a tongue or an interpretation"*? (1 Cor. 14:26)

Clearly, these are important questions for which we must, and I believe we can, find simple answers.

It seems to me that if I were the devil, I would LOVE for well over half of the Body of Christ to be excluded from major areas of ministry!

But how would the Father feel about this?

Would God be satisfied for well over half of the Body of Christ, women, to never fulfill these expectations which certainly seem to apply to ALL believers?

"Go and teach them what I taught you..."

"By this time you ought to be teachers..."

"When you come together, everyone has (something)..."

It certainly seems that God wants "*everyone*," all believers, to be involved in these activities.

It certainly seems that these "*commands*," or instructions, are given to everyone.

It certainly seems that something, *something BIG*, will have to change for these instructions to be fulfilled.

But who has enough influence, enough authority, to initiate this kind of major change?

Chapter Six

Jesus Changed Everything

"But when the time had fully come, God sent his Son..."(Gal. 4:4)

In making this declaration, Paul points to how everything began to change with the coming of Jesus. However, the changes were not intended to move us to something *"new,"* but the beginning of a return to God's original intentions. It was a return to seeing God's great love for all people. A return to seeing God's great desire to build a world-wide family made of every kindred, tribe, and tongue. And a return to understanding that, in Him, genetics do not matter, but the fullness of humanity, male and female, does.

God's View Of Women Has Never Changed-

God's view of women should be clear to all since in the beginning He revealed His own image by creating *"man"* as the combination of *"male and female."* For *"human beings"* to fully and faithfully express the image of God, He had to make *"human"* as both male and female.

> FOR *"HUMAN BEINGS"* TO FULLY AND FAITHFULLY EXPRESS THE IMAGE OF GOD, HE MADE THEM AS BOTH MALE AND FEMALE.

> *"So God created **man** in his own image, in the **image** of God he created him; **male and female he created them**."* (Gen. 1:27)

With the coming of the New Covenant, God's plan to reveal His image by living in and through both men and women, as started in the Garden, begins to gain momentum. God begins to put the spotlight on women by using them in some of the most dramatic ways. This was not dependent on marriage, but on the full expression of male and female. Single people played important roles throughout history! Lest we forget, Paul was single and thought it was a pretty good idea.

> **Good News for Singles**
> It is not marriage that bears the image of God but the full expression of male and female.

God Chose Anna, A Prophetess, To Announce Messiah's Mission.

> *"...(she) spoke about the child to all who were looking forward to the redemption of Jerusalem."* (Luke 2:38)

Some might label this as *"sharing"* or *"giving testimony"* or *"private conversation,"* but it certainly sounds like preaching and teaching to me. Of course, this occurred while still under the Old Covenant. Yet, it sets a clear direction for the way God planned to use women in the extension of His Kingdom through the earthly ministry of Jesus and beyond!

Jesus Had Several Women As Part Of His Inner Circle.

> *"After this, Jesus traveled about from one town and village to another, proclaiming the good news of the kingdom of God. The Twelve were with him, and <u>also some women</u> who had been cured of evil spirits and diseases: <u>Mary</u> (called Magdalene) from whom seven demons had come out; <u>Joanna</u> the wife of Cuza, the manager of Herod's household; <u>Susanna; and many others. These women were helping to support them out of their own means</u>."*
> (Luke 8:1-3)

This was not allowed by any other Jewish teacher or rabbi. Women were never allowed to be *"disciples"* of any recognized rabbinical teacher. Having these women work so closely with Him and the Twelve, on a daily basis, went against every tradition of Jewish society.

When Money Was Involved, The Scandal Was Even Greater-

Some of these women would have been married to wealthy men, widows who had inherited family wealth, and women who were successful in businesses deemed acceptable for women. But using this money to support itinerate teachers would have been scandalous. Obviously, Jesus believed that giving women their rightful place was more important than the opinions of a totally male-dominated society.

> Jesus believed that giving women their rightful place was more important than the opinions of a totally male-dominated society.

Samaritan Woman Becomes A Teacher / Evangelist.

First century Jews viewed *"half-breed, idol-worshipping"* Samaritans as *"dogs,"* lower than Gentiles, because they had intermarried with the surrounding tribes and mixed Judaism with pagan worship. For Jesus to deliberately initiate a spiritual conversation with this disgraced Samaritan woman contradicted serious Jewish prohibitions.

The rabbinic oral law was quite explicit concerning men interacting publicly with women. *"He who talks with a woman [in public] brings evil upon himself."* Another rabbinic teaching prominent in Jesus' day taught, *"One is not so much as to greet a woman."* But the moral condition of this woman made Jesus' interaction with her far more shocking!

It is almost impossible for us, in our culture, to understand the importance of John 4 and what happened after this woman met Jesus.

> *"Then, leaving her water jar, the woman went back to the town and said to the people, 'Come, see a man who told me everything I ever did. Could this be the Christ?' They came out of the town and made their way toward him...<u>Many of the Samaritans from that town believed in him because of the woman's testimony</u>"*
>
> <u>(John 4:28-30, 39)</u>

We can call it *"giving testimony"* or *"sharing,"* but the fact remains, she taught others, men and women, what she had been taught by Jesus. This certainly sounds like preaching and teaching to me.

> **Clearly, Jesus cared far more about elevating women than man-made restrictions and male superiority. He came to see the heart of God demonstrated to all mankind!**

Clearly, Jesus cared far more about elevating women than man-made restrictions and male superiority. As seen in John 3:16, He sought to see the heart of God demonstrated to all mankind! *"God loves the world so much He gave his Son."*

Jesus Blessed Mary For Learning At His Feet-

> *"...Mary, who sat at the Lord's feet listening to what he said... Mary has chosen what is better, and it will not be taken away from her."* <u>(Luke 10:39-42)</u>

This is huge! It was in direct contradiction to the rabbi's view of women being educated; especially alongside men. The separation of *"superior"* men from *"inferior"* women would never have permitted this.

By teaching Mary spiritual truths, Jesus seriously violated other rabbinic laws, which said, "Let the words of the Law be burned rather than taught to women… If a man teaches his daughter the law, it is as though he taught her lechery." (jSot. 3.4; 19a, bSot. 4.3).

Jesus Scandalized The Accepted Male Views Of Women-

The following event was so offensive, on so many levels, not only to all religious leaders, but to all Jewish people. Yet, Jesus never hesitated.

> Now one of the Pharisees invited Jesus to have dinner with him, so he went to the Pharisee's house and reclined at the table. 37 When a woman who had lived a sinful life in that town learned that Jesus was eating at the Pharisee's house, she brought an alabaster jar of perfume, 38 and <u>as she stood behind him at his feet weeping, she began to wet his feet with her tears. Then she wiped them with her hair, kissed them and poured perfume on them.</u> 39 When the Pharisee who had invited him saw this, <u>he said to himself, "If this man were a prophet, he would know who is touching him and what kind of woman she is — that she is a sinner."</u> …44 Then he turned toward the woman and said to Simon, "Do you see this woman? I came into your house. You did not give me any water for my feet, but she wet my feet with her tears and wiped them with her hair. 45 You did not give me a kiss, but this woman, from the time I entered, has not stopped kissing my feet. 46 You did not put oil on my head, but she has poured perfume on my feet. 47 <u>Therefore, I tell you, her many sins have been forgiven — for she loved much.</u> But he who has been forgiven little, loves little." 48 Then Jesus said to her, "Your sins are forgiven." (Luke 7:36-48)

It is nearly impossible for us to understand the scandal this would have caused to ALL accepted customs of first century Jewish, Greek, and Roman culture. Even today, this would appear to be far too sensual to be appropriate in any setting, especially in a church meeting. However, it is difficult to argue with the Son of God's choices in how to relate to the creations He loves so deeply. (*Although Peter did on several occasions. Peter frequently messed up...which always gives me hope.*)

> I can't imagine ANY context where this act would have been acceptable. But it didn't faze Him at all.

Jesus Violated Ritual Impurity Laws To Help Women-

Mark 5:25-34 describes how Jesus was approached by a woman who suffered from menstrual bleeding for 12 years even though the Law was clear that she was unclean, should have been completely avoided, and should have told people she was unclean. She certainly should not have touched anyone, especially a non-relative man.

In fact, she was considered doubly unclean because she touched Him, though she was not His wife or family, and she was bleeding. Yet, Jesus did not hesitate to heal her because of her faith, not her gender.

> *At once Jesus realized that power had gone out from Him. He turned around in the crowd and asked, "Who touched my clothes?" "You see the people crowding against you," his disciples answered, "and yet you can ask, 'Who touched me?'" But Jesus kept looking around to see who had done it. Then the woman, knowing what had happened to her, came and fell at His feet and, trembling with fear, told him the whole truth. He said to her, "Daughter, your faith has healed you. Go in peace and be freed from your suffering."* (Mark 5:30-34)

She *"fell down, trembling with fear."* Why was she so afraid? She knew she had just received a life-changing miracle. Reading this with "church eyes" in the 21st century, we would tend to think she would be thrilled! Like the paralyzed man in Acts 3:8, we would think she would have been *"walking and jumping, and praising God."* However, we would think this way because we don't live in her culture or understand the extreme prejudice she faced every day, in every area of her life, for twelve long years! Prejudices so powerful they were more important than people!

Try to imagine what went through her mind in the moment of this miracle. Jesus suddenly turned around and spoke to the crowd. But He didn't rejoice or say, *"Something wonderful just happened."* Instead, He asked, *"Who touched me?"* She knew the rules. She knew she had seriously violated commandments written 1500 years before, taught daily by the rabbis, and enforced with painful, sometimes deadly consequences.

> **Why would she be so afraid? Because Jewish prejudice was more important than people!**

But Jesus, understanding the true heart and purpose for the Law, ignored the religious leaders and healed her because of her faith, not her gender.

Jesus Used Terminology Which Treated Women Equal To Men-

In **Luke 13:16,** Jesus healed a Jewish woman and called her a *"daughter of Abraham."* Jesus was again causing scandal! The phrase, *"son of Abraham,"* is used several times about Jewish men to honor their genetic connection to the Father of the Faith. But the phrase, *"daughter of Abraham"* is found nowhere else in the Bible, but it does go right back to the equality given man and woman in the Garden.

"Daughter of Abraham" is a designation created by Jesus declaring that women who acted in faith had equal spiritual status with sons of Abraham. No Jewish teacher had ever used this phrase or any others like it because of its clear implication. But when God *"came in flesh,"* He had

no problem declaring that what mattered was not gender or genetics, but simple faith!

God Chose Women To Be First Witnesses To The Resurrection-

> "The angel said to the women...'He is not here; he has risen, just as he said...go quickly and <u>tell his disciples</u>: 'He has risen from the dead and is going ahead of you into Galilee. There you will see him'." (<u>Matt. 28:5-7</u>)

After most of His men ran away, scattered just like He said they would (Mark 14:27), He chose women to be the first people to witness the most amazing, important event since He spoke the worlds into existence! Even more than that, women *became* the witnesses as He sent them to tell His men the very thing He knew they would not believe; *He Has Risen!*

> "When they came back from the tomb, they told all these things to the Eleven and to all the others. It was Mary Magdalene, Joanna, Mary the mother of James, and the others with them who told this to the apostles. But <u>they did not believe the women, because their words seemed to them like nonsense</u>."
> (<u>Luke 24:9-12</u>)

The trust God placed in these women is nearly impossible for us to truly comprehend or fully appreciate. He directly and deliberately contradicted the strongly held and violently enforced Jewish, Greek, and Roman view that women should not be believed, could not make an accusation against a man, and were not allowed to give testimony in court.

Jesus Chose Women To Tell His Disciples What To Do-

> "The women hurried away from the tomb...Suddenly Jesus met

> them. 'Greetings...Do not be afraid. <u>Go and tell my brothers to go to Galilee</u>; there they will see me.'" (Matt. 28:8-10)

In a culture where a woman's testimony was worthless because she was considered worthless, completely untrustworthy, Jesus elevated the value of these women's testimony beyond anything most of the known world had seen before. The people of Jesus' day found this behavior completely unacceptable. His own disciples had been regularly shocked at His behavior and the value He placed on women throughout His ministry. Most notable was when Jesus deliberately travelled through Samaria, an area despised by the Jews, and deliberately had a long conversation with a Samaritan woman whom He knew had serious moral issues. Jesus could have easily avoided Samaria and very easily avoided conversation with this woman. But He did it on purpose.

> "Just then his disciples returned and <u>were surprised to find him talking with a woman.</u> But no one asked, "What do you want?" or "Why are you talking with her?" (John 4:27)

God Didn't Have To Do It This Way-

To witness the Resurrection, He could easily have chosen John, young Mark or any number of respectable, believable Jewish men. Beyond that, He could have easily chosen any of the multitudes of angels to declare the Resurrection just as He used angels to communicate with Abraham, Daniel, or Mary. In fact, an angel ***did*** tell the women at the tomb and they could have just as easily appeared to the men!

But God deliberately chose women to testify to men about the truth of the single greatest act of love, redemption, and divinity- the Resurrection of Christ! God chose women to tell the men. And He did it on purpose!

After reading this overwhelming evidence showing how God feels, and has always felt, about women, I'd be ashamed to feel any different! After all, since Christ is living in us, aren't we supposed to have His mind and His heart, loving what He loves and valuing what He values?

He *CLEARLY* places very high value on women by empowering them for every ministry function possible, as we will see the following chapters.

<u>*How can we do any less?*</u>

> **OF ALL THE OPTIONS AVAILABLE, GOD DELIBERATELY CHOSE WOMEN, AGAIN AND AGAIN!**

Chapter Seven

-Pentecost- Liberation Day For Women!

The New Covenant, Christ living in and through believers, was fully realized on the Day of Pentecost when the Holy Spirit came, not just to temporarily fill or *"visit"*, but to live forever in God's people. (Acts 2) The Day of Pentecost also included a dramatic declaration of liberation for all believing women, for all time. As we read the following verses, imagine the tearing of the cultural fabric by the repeated references both male and female, sons and daughters, *"both men and women."*

The fulfillment of Pentecost is defined in Acts 2:14-18-

> *"Then Peter stood up...raised his voice...this is what was spoken by the prophet Joel: 17 'In the last days, God says, I will pour out my Spirit on <u>all people</u>. Your <u>sons and daughters will prophesy</u>, your young men will see visions, your old men will dream dreams. 18 Even on <u>my servants, both men and women</u>, I will pour out my Spirit in those days, and <u>they will prophesy</u>."*
> (Acts 2:14-18)

We MUST NOT take this declaration lightly! The emphasis on how God was choosing to fill and use *BOTH* men and women equally in the New Covenant was clear and radical, and it was highly offensive to the Jewish leaders in first century Jerusalem. In the hearts and minds of the early disciples this equality changed everything. Especially since Joel's prophecy, which Peter declared was being fulfilled <u>at that very moment</u>; put the emphasis on how the Spirit will fill **both** men and women. And that they (we), both men and women, would be empowered to prophesy, or "*speak the Word of the Lord.*"

This prophecy distinctly specified men and women, not just husbands and wives. The Lord, through Joel, declared His plan for both genders to be His "voice" without regard to marital status. All this was made clear in the message of Pentecost!

> *-God considers BOTH men and women to be His servants.*
> *-God wants to fill BOTH men and women with His Spirit.*
> *-God wants BOTH men and women to <u>speak</u> on His behalf.*

His followers watched Jesus *"change the rules"* for Himself during His earthly ministry. But now, the rules had changed for them, also. The message of Pentecost turned their life-long traditions upside down. The model we see played out in Acts and the Epistles shows that women were forever set free to be fully and freely used by God.

What Was The Divine, Eternal Fulfillment Of Pentecost?

Peter, inspired by the Holy Spirit, declares that the modern day fulfillment of Joel's prophecy is more than just being filled with the Spirit, but also the equality of <u>both men and women</u> to be used by God and to <u>speak</u> on His behalf.

> "*I will pour out my Spirit on* **all people...sons and daughters will prophesy**...*Even on* **my servants,** <u>both</u> **men and women**..."
> (Acts 2:17-18)

The specific wording of Joel's prophecy, and Peter's quoting of these words on Pentecost, makes God's intention very clear-

> –GOD CONSIDERS **BOTH** MEN AND WOMEN TO BE HIS SERVANTS.
>
> –GOD WANTS TO FILL **BOTH** MEN AND WOMEN WITH HIS SPIRIT.
>
> –GOD WANTS **BOTH** MEN AND WOMEN TO <u>SPEAK</u> ON HIS BEHALF.

Seeing that God declared His intention to use **both** men **and** women equally, and reading how Jesus modeled this intention during His earthly ministry; these facts should force us to question how we read later writings of the New Testament. The model we find in the book of Acts demonstrates how they understood Pentecost. Peter, and the other 119 believers in the "upper room," watched how Jesus related to women during His ministry and now they realized the gender liberation that came when people, men AND women, filled with the Spirit.

Wow, this makes Paul's statements about *"women must be silent"* even more difficult to understand. His command to Timothy, *"I do not allow women to teach,"* seems to be completely contradictory to the way Jesus conducted His ministry and God's declaration at Pentecost.

Apparently, we just have to accept that the Word of God, as its critics have claimed, does contain inaccuracies and contradictions. Unless...

Unless, we're wrong.

Unless, we are reading the Bible incorrectly.

Unless, we are mistakenly reading the Bible differently than we read any other written material.

Unless, we are breaking the most simple and basic of all rules regarding the understanding of literature, any literature.

Unless, there is "*more to this story.*"

And, indeed, there is more!

Chapter Eight
Priscilla And Aquila Set The Model Of Pentecost

The husband and wife team of Aquila and Priscilla was very important to the early church. According to accepted guidelines of interpretation, the simple fact that they are mentioned <u>7 times</u> in the New Testament gives a strong indication of their importance.

Being Jewish, this couple would have been strongly influenced by the more rigid male-dominated traditions of first century Judaism. However, they spent much of their time living and ministering in Rome, Corinth and Ephesus where the culture was different in some important ways. For Priscilla and Aquila to fulfill their calling, they had to be willing to allow the Lord to use them to break the cultural mold and blaze a trail for many godly women and men to follow.

This Couple Believed In The Meaning Of Pentecost!

> "After this, Paul left Athens and went to Corinth. There he met a Jew named <u>Aquila</u>, a native of Pontus, who had recently come from Italy with his wife <u>Priscilla</u>, because Claudius had ordered all the Jews to leave Rome. Paul went to see them, and because he was a tentmaker as they were, he stayed and worked with them."
> (Acts 18:1-4)

> "*Paul stayed on in Corinth for some time. Then he left the brothers and sailed for Syria, accompanied by <u>Priscilla and Aquila</u>...They arrived at Ephesus, where Paul left <u>Priscilla and Aquila</u>.*"
>
> (<u>Acts 18:18-22</u>)

First Century Grammatical Norms-

-Although most male leaders were married, not many are listed along with their wives. A major example is Peter whose wife's name is never given. However, the Bible *always* lists Priscilla and Aquila's names together. More importantly, in <u>5 out of 7 times</u>, Priscilla's name is listed first. Is this significant to the way this couple was viewed by other church leaders? Indeed, it was.

Using accepted Greek grammatical guidelines, nearly all Bible scholars believe that Barnabas started out as the leader of their new missionary team as they left Antioch in Acts 13. But shortly after starting on their mission journey, Paul emerges as the accepted leader. Scholars agree on this because, using accepted linguistic norms, Luke began listing Paul's name first.

It would seem unfairly inconsistent to not consider Priscilla and Aquila using the same grammatical guidelines. This would indicate that, though they worked as a team, *Priscilla clearly had the lead role in ministering.*

> **Listing Priscilla's name first, 5 out of 7 times, is a strong indication of leadership.**

The Extremely Influential Training of Apollos-

> "*Meanwhile a Jew named Apollos, a native of Alexandria, came to Ephesus. He was a **learned man, with a thorough knowledge of the Scriptures.** 25 He had been instructed in the way of the*

> Lord, and he spoke with great fervor and taught about Jesus accurately, though he knew only the baptism of John. 26 He began to speak boldly in the synagogue. **When Priscilla and Aquila heard him, they invited him to their home and <u>explained to him the way of God more adequately</u>."**
>
> (Acts 18:24-26)

This is an extremely important passage in helping us understand how the early believers sometimes contradicted cultural norms for the greater good. But Priscilla and Aquila used careful wisdom after meeting an influential Jewish teacher in the Ephesian Jewish synagogue.

Apollos was a highly educated Jew who had been *"converted"* by the ministry of John the Baptist and Jesus. He was a powerful preacher and travelled throughout the Roman Empire teaching in Jewish synagogues about the Messiah. However, he was apparently unaware of what happened on Pentecost, the teaching of the New Covenant and the reality of *"Christ in us."*

When Priscilla and Aquila heard Apollos teach in the synagogue in Ephesus, rather than violate tradition and appear to contradict him, they invited Apollos to their home and *"explained to him the way of God more adequately."* It certainly appears that they did this in a very respectful, careful, and private way.

The Holy Spirit-Inspired Wording Here Is Very Important-

> ***They*** heard him, ***they*** invited them to ***their*** home and ***they*** *"explained to him the way of God more adequately."*

If we look at this situation the same way we view any other story in the Bible, free of preconceived ideas, we can only conclude that this was a couple, with the woman leading, teaching a highly educated Jewish teacher/preacher/leader. Being a wise man, Apollos gratefully submitted to *their* teaching. Priscilla and Aquila served an important role in helping Apollos become a highly regarded apostle whose ministry had great influence in the early church for many years.

This was due, in no small part, to the humility of Apollos as he gratefully received the instruction from BOTH Priscilla and her husband. Apollos was described as a *"learned man, with a thorough knowledge of the Scriptures."* The *"Scripture"* would be the Old Testament. As an expert in the Old Testament, Apollos had no objection to learning from a woman because he understood how God used women throughout history. He knew the first century chauvinistic view was not based on Scripture.

It is also worth noting that, although Apollos was a Jew, he was raised in Alexandria, not Jerusalem. But he did not allow either his Greek culture or his Jewish culture to keep him from receiving critical instruction in the Word of God...from a woman.

> *They* heard him...
> *They* invited him to...
> *Their* home and...
> *They* "explained to him the way of God more adequately."
> **THEY** seem pretty important!

Chapter Nine

Paul's Apostolic "Fellow Workers"

We must be very careful to not place too much meaning on the lack of titles given to women in the Epistles. Why? Because very few men are given titles, either. The early church just didn't title people.

The apostolic writers seldom attached titles to any of the people they greeted in their letters. They used words like *"apostles"* and *"prophets"* as job descriptions, explaining how different people were gifted by the Spirit and how they benefited the Church. Defining a person's gifting is important because when we see the fruit of their gifting, we can release our faith and receive the benefit of their function in the body of Christ.

"Paul, an apostle of Jesus Christ," is very different than, *"The Apostle Paul."* Since Jesus made it painfully clear that no believer in His Kingdom would have rulership over any other believer.

> *"You know that those who are regarded as rulers of the Gentiles lord it over them, and their high officials exercise authority over them. <u>Not so with you</u>. Instead, whoever wants to become great among you must be your servant, and whoever wants to be first must be slave of all."* (Mark 10:42-45)

"<u>Not so with you</u>" Based on His crystal clear commandment, the early Church did not ascribe titles that made one person superior to another since the highest calling was to be a servant to everyone else.

If we are going to be consistent in our Bible study then we must not use a double standard when comparing references to women and men. It's dishonest to do it any other way. And it steals destiny from over half of the body of Christ. So let's take an honest look at the words they used.

> **We must not use a double standard when comparing references to women and men.**

The Most Common "*Title*"-

The most common reference or *"title,"* by far, is to refer to a New Testament leader by their name, and add, *"and the church that meets in their home."* Throughout the Epistles, both men and women are regularly greeted by their name *"and the church that meets in their home."* <u>BOTH men and women.</u>

However, the one title which Paul does use on several occasions when referring to apostolic men and women who worked closely with him is the phrase; *"**fellow workers.**"*

Speaking of the apostolic ministry of himself and Apollos, Paul writes-

> *"For we are God's **fellow workers**; you are God's field, God's building."* (1 Cor. 3:9)

Writing about himself and the others in his apostolic team, Paul says-

> *"As God's **fellow workers** we urge you not to receive God's grace in vain."* (2 Cor. 6:1)

While in a Roman prison, Paul wrote-

> *"My fellow prisoner Aristarchus sends you his greetings, as does Mark, the cousin of Barnabas. (You have received instructions about him; if he comes to you, welcome him.) Jesus, who is called*

> *Justus, also sends greetings. These are the only Jews among my **fellow workers** for the kingdom of God, and they have proved a comfort to me."* (Col. 4:10-11)

Again, writing from prison, Paul uses *"fellow workers"* to refer to leaders well-known for their apostolic gifting and labor-

> *"Epaphras, my fellow prisoner in Christ Jesus, sends you greetings. 24 And so do Mark, Aristarchus, Demas and Luke, my **fellow workers**."* (Philemon 23-24)

Paul acknowledges Priscilla and Aquila's for their labor as his *"fellow-workers"* and pastoral leadership in their local church-

> *"Greet Priscilla and Aquila, my **fellow workers** in Christ Jesus. 4 They risked their lives for me. Not only I but all the churches of the Gentiles are grateful to them. 5 Greet also <u>the church that meets at their house</u>."* (Rom. 16:3-5)

What Did Paul Mean When He Wrote *"Fellow Workers"*?

Paul's use of the words, *"fellow workers,"* is an important indication of apostolic gifting. *"Fellow workers"* means much more than simply co-workers. The Greek words Paul used for <u>fellow workers</u> mean <u>*"equals who are extremely close in union."*</u> Paul used this type of wording only to describe apostolic equals who were the very closest to him and the most highly trusted by him. And as we can see, he uses *"fellow worker"* to describe both men and women.

Paul uses the Greek phrase for *"fellow workers"* when referring to other notable apostolic women who ministered alongside him.

> *"I plead with Euodia and I plead with Syntyche to agree with each other in the Lord. 3 Yes, and I ask you, loyal yokefellow, help these women who have <u>contended at my side in the cause of the gospel</u>, along with Clement and the rest of my **fellow workers**, whose names are in the book of life."* (Phil.4:2-3)

Paul's use of the *"fellow workers"* designation for certain gifted women is even more important when we realize how women were considered of little or no importance throughout most of the Empire. Writing about them as his *fellow workers*, *"equals who are extremely close in union"* with him, was a huge departure from the current culture.

> The Greek phrase for *"fellow workers"* means *"equals who are extremely close in union."* Paul used this type of wording only to describe apostolic equals. And he used it for men AND women.

If these women were to stay silent, have no input, and do no teaching, why would Paul use very important space in a first century letter to *"plead"* with them to walk in agreement? Paul shows the leadership roles these women held by his strong command for the local leaders to give them all the help they needed for the *"<u>cause of the gospel</u>."*

To be consistent, we must believe this specific wording was inspired by the Holy Spirit. The only logical reason this specific wording would be chosen by the Spirit is because of God's desire to flow in and through all who belong to Christ, without regard to gender or genetics. Seeing how God used women in the New Covenant, it's becoming clear that in regards to both salvation and gifting, there truly is neither male nor female in Christ Jesus.

> APOSTOLIC "FELLOW WORKERS,"
> MALE AND FEMALE,
> REGULARLY LABORED SIDE BY SIDE WITH PAUL

> There is neither Jew nor Greek, slave nor free, male nor female, for you are all one in Christ Jesus. If you belong to Christ, then you are Abraham's seed, and heirs according to the promise.
> Gal. 3:28-29

Chapter Ten

Paul's Value For Women in Leadership

The book of Acts and the Epistles make it very clear that women were essential to the founding of the Church and its spread throughout the Roman Empire. Though, as we will see, God gave temporary, localized instructions depending on the culture, women served in virtually every capacity in the early church without regard to their gender. They did so with faith, humility and the power of the Holy Spirit. And for the past two thousand years, women like these have been a primary moving force in nearly every church, charity, humanitarian and missionary effort around the world.

Is Paul the Bad Guy?

For nearly all those two thousand years, the apostle Paul has been accused of being a male chauvinist and permanently documented that chauvinistic view in his Epistles. Nothing could be further from the truth. Ignoring context, choosing to not compare Scripture with Scripture and using an inconsistent standard of interpretation has been *"putting words in Paul's mouth"* for hundreds of years. So let's read his words for ourselves and see how Paul speaks about women, their role in the churches and in his specific ministry.

> Ignoring context, choosing to not compare Scripture with Scripture and using an inconsistent standard of interpretation has been *"putting words in Paul's mouth"* for hundreds of years.

"*Work Hard in the Lord*"-

As much as the Scripture honors the work of what we would call, *"stay-at-home moms,"* when Paul makes multiple references to women who *"work hard in the Lord,"* he was not referring to them. Paul had high honor and much praise for those who cooked meals, cleaned house and had babies. But these women were singled out by name for such high honor for a different reason.

Paul honored certain women by name, just as he honored certain men by name, not by bestowing lofty titles, but for their hard work in spreading the Gospel, planting churches throughout the Roman Empire; and discipling many in the New Covenant.

> Women who "*work hard in the Lord*" did far more than just the dishes!

> "Greet <u>Tryphena</u> and <u>Tryphosa</u>, those **women who work hard in the Lord**. Greet my dear friend <u>Persis</u>, **another woman who has worked very hard in the Lord**. 13 Greet Rufus, chosen in the Lord, and **his mother**, who has been a mother to me, too."
> (Rom. 16:12-13)

> "Greet <u>Mary</u>, **who worked very hard for you**."   (Rom. 16:6)

Chloe, Doctrine and Sinful Behavioral-

Chloe and other leaders in her church wrote Paul about doctrinal and behavioral problems in the churches in Corinth.

> "My brothers, some from **Chloe's household** have informed me that there are quarrels among you."   (1 Cor. 1:11)

When men are listed with a church in their house, they are consistently viewed as the pastor/leader of that group. There are no exceptions made for the numerous times when women are listed in the same way. Scripture lists several women as having a *"church in their house."*

It is a serious violation of biblical integrity to insist that these women were not pastors or leaders when they had a "*church in their house,*" just as the men. There is no basis to claim that in a woman's case, she was not the leader, but the church simply met in her house unless we hold this position for men, also.

In the case of Paul's writing what we refer to as 1 Corinthians, it was Chloe and believers in her house church who raised the relational, behavioral, and doctrinal questions which they sent to Paul for explanation and instruction. We do not know what those exact questions were but we know that 1 Corinthians was Paul's response to *"Chloe and the church in her house."*

> **When Scripture lists men with a *"church in their house,"* they are viewed as the pastor. Why would it be any different when women are listed with a *"church in their house?"***

It would be a grossly dishonest interpretation to view men listed with a *"church in their home"* as the pastoral leader but not consider women in the same role with the same description as serving in the same capacity!

Seeing the honor with which Paul and the other apostles addressed these women leaders, we should be ashamed for the way other leaders over the centuries have done just the opposite. By using isolated verses, rejecting both context and culture, far too many men have kept women as second-class citizens in the Kingdom of God for over seventeen hundred years. This most clearly is not what Jesus and the first apostles intended!

Philip's Notable Daughters-

Philip had four daughters whose ministry gifts were exceptional enough to be uniquely mentioned by Luke in the historical narrative of Acts.

> "Leaving the next day, we reached Caesarea and stayed at the house of Philip the evangelist, one of the Seven. 9 <u>He had four unmarried daughters who prophesied.</u>" (Acts 21:8-9)

Since Paul taught that *"all may prophesy"* (1 Cor.14:31), we can be assured that prophecy was very common in the early church. But, for Luke to go out of his way to point out Philip's four daughters for their ministry of prophesying certainly indicates that they operated in more than just the gift of prophecy, but were prominent as prophets or *"prophetesses."*

John Wrote Scripture To An Honored Woman-

If the early Church practice was to keep women silent in church gatherings and from ever teaching men, it seems very bizarre that the Holy Spirit would inspire John to write an important portion of Holy Scripture to a *"chosen lady...and her children."* John opens the second letter we have with this-

> **How Dare John Write God's Holy Word To A Woman**

> "The elder, to the <u>chosen lady and her children</u>, whom I love in the truth, and not I only, but also all who know the truth."
>
> (2 John 1)

John ends his letter with greetings from the church he is living with at the time of this writing, and the female leader-

"The children of your chosen sister send their greetings." (2 John 13)

After all the different ways we have read women referred to, described, and honored, just like their male counterparts; now we see a portion of Scripture addressed specifically to a woman leading a church!

In all honesty, don't we have to admit that whatever he meant, Paul could not have meant, *"All women keep silent in all churches?"*

> **It would be a grossly dishonest interpretation to view men listed with a "*church in their home*" as pastoral leaders but not consider women in the same role, with the same description, as serving in the same leadership capacity!**

Chapter Eleven

Phoebe, Romans And Teaching Men

Paul's letter to the believers in Rome is unique among his epistles. Every other Pauline letter we have was written to either a church Paul had planted or to a person he knew well. But the epistle to the Romans was written to a group of churches Paul did not plant. He had not yet been to Rome, he was planning to go, and the purpose of his letter was to give a full explanation of what he called *"my gospel"* before he arrived. His hope was that when he did go to Rome, his trip would be more fruitful if they already understood his message.

Obviously, the most important requirement for the person who was chosen to deliver any of these letters was the ability to read, and read well. That may seem obvious to us, but remember; only approximately 3% of the people living in the first century were able to read. Any one chosen to deliver an apostolic letter would have been a rarity in the first century; an educated person who was capable of reading to, and teaching, others. Why? Because the ability to just read would not be enough.

Giving understanding of the truth taught in the epistles was the point of writing them. The rare ability to read, and the ability to answer questions on doctrine, was highly

> **The rare ability to read and the ability to answer questions on doctrine was highly valued in the early church.**

valued in the early church. So whoever delivered an apostolic letter would be expected to answer the numerous important questions that would surely be asked and explain the more difficult portions of the writing.

It would be ridiculous to think that Paul would send someone on a long and dangerous journey to deliver some of the most important truth in the world, only to have that person respond to the many questions that would surely come, with *"Sorry, you know I have to stay silent in this meeting because I am a woman. But I'd be happy to talk with the women after the service."* The very idea is silly; it makes no sense.

**So, who did Paul choose to deliver this important letter and make sure the Roman believers clearly understood its truths?
<u>A WOMAN!</u>**

*"I commend to you our sister **Phoebe**, a servant of the church in Cenchrea. I ask you to receive her in the Lord in a way worthy of the saints and to give her any help she may need from you, for she has been a great help to many people, including me."* (Rom. 16:1-2)

Why Paul Chose Phoebe-

Paul was in the Corinthian area when he wrote this letter and chose one of the trusted women named Phoebe, to deliver it to the believers in Rome. Phoebe was a leader in the church in Cenchrea, a port area outside of Corinth. We know she was a church leader because of Paul's use of the Greek word,

> It's just silly to think Paul would send someone on a long, dangerous journey to deliver the world's most important truth, only to have that person respond to questions with, *"Sorry, you know I can't answer that because I'm a woman."*

"diakonos." Remember, *"diakonos"* is the Greek word that is translated *"deacon or minister."* In Acts 6, when seven men were chosen to make sure the widows were taken care of, the Greek word used to describe them was a form of *"diakonos."*

Stephen and Philip were two of the seven chosen to serve in this capacity. As part of their serving in the church, they became well known for their preaching and teaching. These seven men were never formally titled *"deacons,"* but as the Church spread throughout the Empire, *"diakonos"* became a more formal designation as we see later in Paul's use of it in **1 Timothy 3**.

-Paul Had No Problem Referring To Phoebe As *"Deacon."*

"Diakonos" is also translated as *"servant"* and *"minister or ministry."* Each time we see the words *"deacon, servant or minister"* it is a form of the same word. When the New Testament refers to women *"serving or ministering,"* they are in fact *"deaconing."* The original language is very clear. However, due to generations of male dominance, few translators have been willing to refer to women as deacons. Paul, however, had no problem referring to Phoebe as *"a 'deacon' of the church in Cenchrea."*

When he introduced her to the believers in Rome, he used the most honoring language possible to insure that the believers would openly and completely receive her as the leader God had made her. More importantly, Paul wanted to insure they would listen to her, fully believe she carried the truth of this *"mysterious"* New Covenant; and receive her as one who had the authority and the ability to answer the important questions they would no doubt be asking. A huge responsibility! But Paul chose her with no apology or explanation. None was needed because this was normal behavior in the early church.

Along with this most glowing introduction, Paul gave no special command for Phoebe to teach and answer questions only from women. Paul honored Phoebe in the same way he wrote about his most trusted men. Surely, she was sent to do more than simply *"keep silent."*

Paul's introduction and injunction to help Phoebe in <u>*every way possible*</u> is a strong indicator of how much she was valued and trusted. This recommendation of a woman, without the mention of a husband, is one of the most honoring in all of Paul's letters. Its importance cannot be over-stated since Paul entrusted Phoebe with transmitting the most important truths in the world. Listen to the amazing trust in Paul's words spoken about a woman being sent to, of all places, Rome.

> *-"I commend to you our sister Phoebe,*
> *-A servant (deacon) of the church in Cenchrea.*
> *-Receive her in the Lord,*
> *-In a way worthy of the saints.*
> *-Give her any help she may need from you.*
> *-She has been a great help to many people,*
> *-including me."* <u>(Rom. 16:1-2)</u>

> This recommendation of a woman, without the mention of a husband, is one of the most honoring in all of Paul's letters.
>
> Its importance cannot be over-stated since Paul entrusted Phoebe with transmitting the most important truths in the world, in one of the most male-dominated places in the world, the city of Rome.

Can Women Be Apostolic?

This is probably the hardest question of all because it deals with foundational issues in the Church. However, I believe that once we understand the way women are truly pictured in the totality of the Epistles, it becomes simple to see the original model in the early Church.

Priscilla and Aquila are clearly described as apostles, doing apostolic work, planting churches, and training other apostles throughout Asia and Italy. We have seen several verses where Paul used language that certainly describes apostolic gifting in several other women, including some of his female relatives.

> "Greet Andronicus and **Junias**, my relatives who have been in prison with me. **They are outstanding among the apostles**, and they were in Christ before I was." (Rom. 16:7)

This wording clearly designates Junias, and her husband, as apostles. Any other meaning would have been written, *"They are considered to be outstanding **by** the apostles."*

The language we saw earlier in Phil. 4:2-3, shows that Paul included Euodia and Syntyche in his designation of ***"fellow workers,"*** which clearly refers to their apostolic gifting and function. If these women had to be silent and not teach, why use valuable space to encourage their unity and future work in *"the cause of the Gospel"*?

> *"I plead with Euodia and I plead with Syntyche to agree with each other in the Lord. Yes, and I ask you, loyal yokefellow, help these women who have contended at my side in the cause of the gospel, along with Clement and the rest of my fellow workers..."*
>
> (Phil. 4:2-3)

When we consider the level of responsibility Paul gave to women such as Phoebe, Priscilla, Junia, Chloe, Euodia, Syntyche and so many others, it's just not possible to equate these amazing women with the ones to whom Paul wrote, *"Keep quiet, don't speak, don't teach men."*

But Paul did write those things.

Clearly, he was not referring to these women.

So who could he have been referring to and why?

Chapter Twelve

Did Paul Intend To Be Contradictory?

Paul was a brilliant thinker. He spent his teen years as one of the few disciples of the celebrated Torah expert, Gamaliel. He devoted his entire life to a mastery of the sacred texts delivered to the people of God over the many generations from Moses to Malachi. And yet, he gave the last half of his life to helping people gain an understanding of the *"simplicity of Christ"* as revealed in those same sacred texts, what we call the Old Testament. (2 Cor. 11:3-6)

We can't know to what extent the early apostles realized they, too, were writing more *"sacred text."* But they did have an understanding that some of their letters were more than temporary communication. Peter, writing about how some were twisting Paul's letters, stated, *"...which ignorant and unstable people distort, as they do the **other Scriptures**..."* (2 Peter 3:16)

This simple statement makes it clear these men had some understanding that their words were more than just *"their words."*

Simple And Clear-

What we can be certain of is that Paul labored to make his message simple and clear. A passionate, brilliant man writing to an uneducated audience who, almost always, would have to have the courier read the letter to them; Paul would have labored on their behalf to be simple and clear. Knowing that most of his audience were Gentiles who would have little knowledge of the "*Old Testament*," Paul would have labored even more to be simple and clear. He put his trust in the transforming power of God's grace instead of the complicated thinking and legal wrangling of the Pharisees with whom he had been trained.

> *"For Christ did not send me to baptize, but to preach the gospel — <u>not with words of human wisdom</u>, lest the cross of Christ be emptied of its power."* (1 Cor. 1:17)

> *"My message and my preaching were <u>not with wise and persuasive words</u>, but with a demonstration of the Spirit's power, so that your faith might not rest on men's wisdom, but on God's power."* (1 Cor. 2:4-5)

It's Not Simple Or Clear To Me!

We can be sure Paul did not intend to be complicated and contradictory since he was laboring to communicate the literal "*words of life*." And yet, 2000 years later, it can certainly seem to be anything but simple or clear. That is, unless we constantly remind ourselves to follow the simple rules of understanding we use with all other literature we read. This is especially true when reading things written long ago and in vastly different cultures.

Paul tells the believers in Corinth concerning the confusion they were having in their meetings that women, as well as men, are to pray and prophesy when the church meets together:

> "...**every woman** who prays or prophesies..." (1 Cor. 11:5)

-But three chapters later, he writes:

> "...women should remain **silent** in the churches. They are not allowed to speak... for it is disgraceful **for a woman to speak** in the church." (1 Cor. 14:34-35)

-Wait a minute. Just nine verses earlier he had written:

> "<u>When you come together,</u> **everyone** has a hymn, or **a word of instruction**, a revelation, a tongue or an interpretation." (1 Cor. 14:26)

> "For you can **all prophesy** in turn so that **everyone may be instructed** and encouraged. The spirits of prophets are subject to the control of prophets. 33 For God is not a God of disorder but of peace." (1 Cor. 14:31-33)

-And yet again, Paul seems to completely contradict what we just read when he sends instruction to his son-in-the-faith, Timothy, who was the overseer of the churches in and around Ephesus.

(Ephesus will be important when we address culture and local instructions)

> "A woman must quietly receive instruction with entire submissiveness. But I do not allow a woman **to teach or exercise** (usurp, take unlawfully) **authority** over a man, but to **remain quiet**." (1 Tim. 2:11-13 NASB)

Are we to believe that the Holy Spirit would inspire Paul to so blatantly contradict himself when writing instructions on something as important as how over half of Christ's community (women) should behave when acting in His name? Whenever we find a place where the Scripture *"seems"* to completely contradict itself, don't we have a solemn responsibility to keep asking, *"Is there more to this story?"*

-Absolute Truth and Apparent Contradictions-

"There must be more to this story."

We know the law of gravity is an absolute truth. So when we see a child let go of a balloon and it goes up instead of down, we do not now disbelieve the law of gravity. When we watch a huge piece of metal weighing over 100 tons picking up speed on a runway and then lifting off the asphalt to soar over 30,000 feet above the ground, none of us decide that apparently the law of gravity no longer exists, having somehow been done away with. Instead, we simply think, *"There is obviously more information which I don't yet have."*

"I won't decide yet because there has to be more to this story."

Paul understood that in Christ, there was to be no distinction made by genetics or gender; no Jew or Gentile, no slave or free, no male or female. (Gal. 3:28) He fully believed this both in salvation, and in how the gifts of the Spirit work through God's people, without regard to genetics, gender, or social standing.

> **When we see a balloon float up instead of fall down, we don't stop believing in gravity. We know there must be more to the story.**

However, Paul also had a unique sensitivity and understanding of how local culture and tradition could **help** or **hinder** the spread of the Gospel. And he sought, by any means possible, to reach as many as possible. His temporary instructions were aimed directly at not hindering the Gospel. Here's some *"more to this story."*

Chapter Thirteen

Cultural Norms, Localized Instructions And Eternal Truth

A simple, logical reading of biblical instructions shows that some of them were given because of localized, cultural issues; AND they all contain eternal truth. All are true, but some were temporary. Though God's truth is eternal, some of His instructions on how to live out that truth were temporary; and this is true from Genesis to Revelation.

True, but Temporary

True, but temporary applies to many biblical circumstances, from collecting manna in the wilderness every morning (except Saturdays), which was governed by very strict temporary commandments, the violation of which could bring stoning, but ended when they entered the promised land (Ex.16-Joshua 5); to not eating ceremonial unclean food, which was forbidden in the Old Testament but ended when Christ came. *("In saying this, Jesus declared all foods 'clean'."* Mark 7:19 NIV) In other words; some instructions were true, but temporary.

The Holy Scriptures are replete with commands and instructions that were divine, given by God, with serious results if disobeyed; AND were also temporary and only for one location, one period of time or one group of people. Again, true, but temporary.

It's not too difficult for the average Christian to see this *"true, but temporary"* understanding as it applies to the Old Testament *"ceremonial"* laws; but harder to understand how it applies in the New Testament. However, the principle and practice is the same. And when read in context, comparing Scripture with other Scripture, and a little understanding of 2000 year old culture, it becomes easier to see the temporary aspect of some New Testament instructions.

> **Regardless of how we choose to interpret Scripture, we must be consistent. Integrity demands that we not pick some and ignore others.**

If we choose to interpret all Scripture in a wooden, literal, permanent fashion, then we have a divine duty to remain consistent. We must faithfully obey <u>*all*</u> New Testament commands and apply them <u>*all*</u>, to <u>*all*</u> Christians, <u>*all*</u> the time and in <u>*all*</u> places. Just in the handful of passages we are looking at regarding women's roles in leadership, we must judge for ourselves, based on a wooden, literal, isolated view of Scripture, if we and our churches are truly *"obeying"* the Word of God.

<u>Here are some New Testament commands we must *"literally"* obey:</u>

1) All women must never wear jewelry; gold, silver, pearls, etc.
2) All women must wear inexpensive clothes.
3) All women must have long hair.
4) All women must never braid their hair.
5) All women must always wear head scarves to pray or prophesy.
6) All women must pray and prophesy, but do it silently.
7) All men must never wear a hat when they pray or prophesy, including baseball caps, cowboy hats, or caps with Scripture verses.
8) All men must always lift their hands when they pray; even Baptists.

9) All men must never have long hair (*even though most Jewish men did have long hair because of rabbinical commands*).

10) Every man is the *"head"* over every woman; universally, not just within marriage. This should result in no man working a job where a woman is superior. *(Or renouncing our USA citizenship if a woman is elected president.)*

11) Every woman must stay completely silent, from the time a church meeting begins, to the time it ends; complete silence.

12) If a woman wants to learn anything about God's Word, she must ask only her husband, and ask only at home.

13) Every church must have a "widow's list" with detailed rules about who gets financial help from the church and who doesn't, including the washing of the feet of the saints.

And finally, the personal favorite of many unmarried guys-

14) Everyone, in every church meeting, must kiss everyone else, every time they meet. (*This is commanded* **5 times** *in the Epistles.*)

Are These Temporary, Localized Instructions or Permanent, Worldwide Commandments?

The Epistles contain all of the above commands. But they don't contain instruction that tells us they are to be viewed as temporary; limited to the culture and time in which the writer lived.

However, the overwhelming majority of Christians view these commands as temporary and do not practice them today. In fact, none of us actually takes *every word* of the Bible to be absolutely literal to us, today, no matter how much we may pretend we do.

If there are not some temporary, cultural instructions in the New Testament, then why don't we obey each of these clear commands?

We Must Always Greet Each Other with a Kiss-

This command seems to be very important since it was written in five different Epistles by both Peter and Paul, to all the churches.

"Greet one another with a holy kiss."	(Rom. 16:16)
"Greet one another with a holy kiss."	(1 Cor. 16:20)
"Greet one another with a holy kiss."	(2 Cor. 13:12)
"Greet all the brothers with a holy kiss."	(1 Thess. 5:26)
"Greet one another with a kiss of love."	(1 Peter 5:14)

Men, *Everywhere,* Must Lift Up Their Hands When Praying-

>"I want men **everywhere** to lift up holy hands in prayer, without anger or disputing." (1 Tim. 2:8)

Paul seems to be very clear in his instructions concerning how men are supposed to pray, always with hands lifted, *everywhere*, no exceptions.

No Braided Hair, Gold, Pearls or Expensive Clothes-

>"I also want women to dress modestly, with decency and propriety, **not with** braided hair or gold or pearls or expensive clothes, but with good deeds, appropriate for women who profess to worship God." (1 Tim. 2:9-10)

>"Your adornment **must not be** merely external — braiding the hair, and wearing gold jewelry, or putting on dresses..."
>(1 Peter 3:3 NASB)

If we forbid braided hair, expensive clothes, silver, gold and pearls, we could raise a lot of money with church "garage" sales!

Silence in Church, Questions Only to Husbands, Only at Home-

> *"As in all the congregations of the saints, women should **remain silent** in the churches. They are **not allowed to speak**, but must be in submission, as the Law says. If they want to inquire about something, they should **ask their own husbands** at **home**; for it is **disgraceful** for a **woman to speak in the church**."*
>
> (1 Cor. 14:33-35)

Men over Women, No Hats for Men, Head Covered for Women-

> *"Now I want you to realize that the head of **every man** is Christ, and the **head of the woman** is man, and the head of Christ is God. **Every man who prays** or prophesies with his head covered dishonors his head. And **every woman who prays** or prophesies with her head uncovered dishonors her head — it is just as though her head were shaved. If a woman does not cover her head, she should have her hair cut off; and if it is a disgrace for a woman to have her hair cut or shaved off, she should cover her head."*
>
> (1 Cor. 11:3-6)

"If a woman does not cover her head, she should have her hair cut off..." I know it's become very popular for churches, large and small, to have a coffee shop for its attendees. But how many churches have volunteer beauticians to cut women's hair so they can pray or prophesy?

> *(There were very good reasons to have instructions about women's hair in the first century, as we will see later.)*

A Widows' List in Every Church-

According to the apostles teaching from the early days after Pentecost, through the founding of churches across the Empire, each church was to have a widow list with very specific rules and requirements to provide financial support. How many churches obey this command today?

> "The church should care for any widow who has no one else to care for her...7 <u>Give these instructions</u> to the church so that the widows you support will not be criticized...9 A widow who is <u>put on the list</u> for support must be a woman who is at least sixty years old...10 She must be well respected by everyone because of the good she has done...<u>Then the church can care for widows who are truly alone.</u>" (1 Tim. 5:3-16 NLT)

Is it possible that Paul's instructions concerning each church caring for their widows no longer apply in the same way because of Social Security, Medicare, pensions, retirements accounts, IRAs , etc.?
The culture has changed. Have the instructions changed?

Everyone Must Speak in Every Meeting-

> "When you come together, **everyone** has a hymn, or a word of instruction, a revelation, a tongue or an interpretation...for the strengthening of the church." (1 Cor. 14:26)

Everyone must speak or lead a song in every service. That sounds fine in a living room, but how is that going to work in a small church of 100 people? Or 1,000 people? Or 10,000 people?

Wow, we are going to have some long meetings!

Offerings Are To Be Collected And Sent To Jerusalem Churches-

> "Now about the <u>collection for God's people:</u> Do what I told the Galatian churches to do. 2 On the first day of every week, each one of you should set aside a sum of money in keeping with his

income, saving it up, so that when I come no collections will have to be made. 3 Then, when I arrive, I will give letters of introduction to the men you approve and send them with your gift to Jerusalem." (1 Cor. 16:1-3)

Today, we have modified the original intent of passages like these, (*2 Cor. 8, 9 and others*) and now use them to teach about giving offerings for the building and maintaining of the local church, missions, etc. And we should.

Why? Because we understand that the instruction to help the starving believers in Jerusalem was a cultural and temporary command. But the principle of generously giving for the care of churches, the care of people, and the spreading of the Gospel is the eternal purpose in Paul's teaching to the Corinthians, and to us.

Different Location, Different Culture, Different Rules

My wife, Linda, turned 16 while living in St. Louis, Missouri, got her driver's licenses, and began driving. A few months later her family moved to New Jersey and she had to stop driving because the driving age in New Jersey was 17. It didn't matter that she already had a driver's licenses or that she had been legally driving for months. Different location, different culture, different rules.

To make matters even more confusing, the alcohol drinking age in New Jersey was 21. But just a few miles across the river in New York, the legal drinking age was just 18. So every weekend there was a constant stream of 18, 19, and 20 year olds scurrying across the bridge into New York City so they could legally indulge. Probably not very safe, but different location, different culture, different rules.

If a westerner spent any time in Asia, they would notice a cultural issue the first time they went out to eat in some of the local cafes. In many places, the customers eat with their fingers, often from common plates. However, they don't wash their hands BEFORE the meal. But they do wash AFTER the meal. Different locations, different customs, and apparently, different immune systems! Carry lots of hand sanitizer and maybe ask for a separate plate.

> **Temporary, cultural, and localized commands all contain eternal truth.**
>
> **It just takes common sense to see how to apply it in our day.**

Chapter Fourteen

Temporary, Cultural Instructions For The Greater Good

A fair and sensible reading of the book of Acts and Epistles shows that Paul's absolute position on the truth of salvation by faith in Christ alone, the mystery and miracle of the New Covenant of *"Christ in you,"* and transforming power of true grace was never compromised. But, he also had a glorious obsession to make sure no non-essential issue hindered the spread of the Gospel to every *"tribe, tongue and culture."* To accomplish this divine commission, Paul frequently made concessions over non-essentials in order to get the Gospel to every place and everyone possible.

Cultural Concessions for the Spread of the Good News-

As the early church spread throughout the Empire, the believers were taught to not be offensive over non-essential things so that they could reach more people and extend the Kingdom. Asian believers understood Paul was a Jew and had been raised in the most strict, most unyielding sect, the Pharisees. But the transformation which the in-dwelling Christ made in this former Pharisee enabled Paul to lay aside his former obsession with *"jot and tittle"* issues and set the model of *"concessions in non-essentials"* for the early believers, both Jew and Gentile.

In giving instructions about choosing local church leaders, Paul was concerned that the candidates had to be viewed by unbelievers as being people of true integrity.

> "...so that those who oppose you may be ashamed because they have <u>nothing bad to say about us</u>."   (Titus 2:8)

> "He must also have <u>a good reputation with outsiders</u>, so that he will not fall into disgrace and into the devil's trap."   (1 Tim. 3:7)

Slavery in the first century was very different from what most of us think of as *"slavery."* Certainly there were people who were in slavery due to being part of a conquered people. But most first century slavery was actually due to overwhelming debt, making them *"bond-servants."* It was still a miserable life that demanded unquestioning obedience while working, but it was a common and critical part of the culture across the Empire.

Even though the apostles were certainly against slavery, and the total control of any one person over another, they understood that it was part of the culture. Rather than simply say, *"This isn't right,"* they taught those in slavery to live a life of honor and obedience to their masters that even non-believers would admire.

> *"Teach slaves to be subject to their masters in everything, to try to please them, not to talk back to them, and not to steal from them, but to show that they can be fully trusted, <u>so that in every way they will make the teaching about God our Savior</u> **<u>attractive</u>**."*   (Titus 2:9-10)

Should We Work to Make the Gospel Attractive?

> *"...so that in every way they will make the teaching about God our Savior **attractive**."*   (Titus 2:10)

Paul's teaching that we should live so that the quality of our lives will be attractive to the lost, was not some kind of *"gimmick"* to hook people, making them think that serving Jesus would somehow make them more *"attractive"* and all their problems go away.

> **Making the Gospel "attractive" through godly character was not a gimmick, but a wise way to communicate divine truth.**

Rather, it was intended to communicate the abundant life found only in Christ. It is a testimony to the validity of the transforming power of the Gospel to *"attract or draw"* people because of the quality of life in Christ. Simply put, when Christ comes by His Spirit to live in and through a person, then loving, unselfish and godly attributes begin to be seen in them; and that kind of life attracts hurting people.

> *"For women who claim to be devoted to God should make themselves __attractive__ by the good things they do."*
>
> (1 Tim. 2:10 NLT)

In this instruction, Paul was certainly not giving fashion advice to believing women. But he was encouraging them to live in such a way that they would give hope to struggling people and draw them to Christ through the good works they did for others.

Paul's Purpose in Making Some Non-Essential Concessions-

To the Corinthians, to whom Paul had given instructions about women not teaching and wearing head coverings, he also gave the reason for why he gave certain commands. Though these instructions made no difference in their righteousness before God, they did affect how unbelievers might respond to the Gospel. Paul desperately wanted the

Corinthian believers to see that spreading the Gospel is a much higher goal then their own personal cultural liberties.

> "Though I am free and belong to no man, I make myself a slave to everyone, <u>to win as many as possible</u>. To the Jews I became like a Jew, <u>to win the Jews</u>. To those under the law I became like one under the law (though I myself am not under the law), <u>so as to win</u> those under the law. 21 To those not having the law I became like one not having the law (though I am not free from God's law but am under Christ's law), <u>so as to win</u> those not having the law. 22 To the weak I became weak, <u>to win</u> the weak. I have become all things to all men so that <u>by all possible means</u> I might save some. 23 <u>I do all this for the sake of the gospel,</u> that I may share in its blessings." (1 Cor. 9:19-23)

As a freeborn Roman citizen, highly educated and widely travelled, Paul had a great appreciation of different cultures, values, and traditions. As we see, Paul's highest goal was <u>to reach as many as possible</u> with the Gospel. He never made concessions that violated the truth of Christ but he did make concessions over non-essentials in order to gain on open door for the Gospel.

> **Why was Paul willing to observe certain traditions he did not believe had any value?**

Why Would Paul Follow Certain Jewish Traditions?

This helps explain why, though he preached so adamantly against trusting in the Law for salvation and righteousness, Paul had no problem on some occasions making concessions concerning both Jewish and pagan customs.

As strongly as Paul fought against those who taught salvation by keeping the Law; he fought just as strongly against turning non-essentials into roadblocks to the Gospel. He fully understood that the Gospel itself was already a *"stone of stumbling and rock of offense."*

Following any Jewish traditions could have been a major roadblock for Paul, himself, since he referred to all the Jewish things he did in the past, hoping to please God, as *"rubbish."* (Phil. 3:4-8)

Timothy Was Circumcised, Titus Was Not-

Paul firmly believed that circumcision was wrong if one trusted it for salvation. However, in order to not offend the Jews unnecessarily, Paul had Timothy circumcised when he added him to the apostolic team.

> *"There was a young disciple named Timothy. His mother was a Jewish believer, but his father was a Greek...Paul wanted him to join them on their journey. In deference to the Jews of the area, he arranged for Timothy to be circumcised before they left*
> (Acts 16:1-4 NLT)

But when Paul went back to Jerusalem in Acts 15, Titus was part of his team and was not circumcised.

> *"Yet not even Titus, who was with me, was compelled to be circumcised..."* (Gal. 2:3)

What was the difference? The text and context tells us. Timothy was half Jewish. Paul had him circumcised so the Jews could not claim that he taught Jews to completely betray their culture. But Titus was fully Greek and had no need of circumcision since he did not convert to Judaism.

Paul Took Some Jewish Vows-

> *"Before he sailed, he had his hair cut off at Cenchrea because of a vow he had taken. They arrived at Ephesus, where Paul left*

> *Priscilla and Aquila. He himself went into the synagogue and <u>reasoned with the Jews</u>."* (Acts 18:18-20)

Why would Paul do that? Again, the context gives us an idea; so he would have a better chance of getting the Jews to listen to the Gospel.

When Paul returned to Jerusalem in Acts 21, the apostles told him of the great number of Jews who were now believers, and also of the accusations that were being made against him. For the sake of keeping peace, they asked him to do something that, for Paul, was fairly extreme. But he did it out of love and peace.

> *"Here's what we want you to do. We have four men here who have completed their vow. Go with them to the Temple and join them in the purification ceremony, paying for them to have their heads ritually shaved. Then everyone will know that the rumors are all false..."* (Acts 21:23-24)

Some years later, after he was arrested and was now being taken for trial in Rome, Paul referred that occasion when making his defense before Felix, the Roman Governor. He had no problem referring to the offerings he made in the Temple and that he had followed the Jewish ritual to be considered ceremonially clean.

> *"After an absence of several years, I came to Jerusalem to bring my people gifts for the poor and to <u>present offerings</u>. <u>I was ceremonially clean</u> when they found me in the temple courts doing this. There was no crowd with me, nor was I involved in any disturbance."* (Acts 24:17-19)

Remember, Paul observed these Jewish customs even though he knew, and taught others, that the Temple was no longer the House of God, the building was empty and God now lived in every believer, and that the offerings made there were no more holy than offerings given anywhere else. But he did these things because they were nonessentials and he sincerely wanted to make peace so the Gospel could be heard. He paid a huge price for his concessions and they didn't always work. But he knew it was God's will and he acted out of love for the lost!

Paul Made Concessions To Reach Gentiles-

> "To those not having the law I became like one not having the law (though I am not free from God's law but am under Christ's law), so as to win those not having the law…I have become all things to all men so that <u>by all possible means</u> I might save some. <u>I do all this for the sake of the gospel</u>, that I may share in its blessings." (1 Cor. 9:19-23)

For a Jew, what to eat and what not to eat were major issues. No pork, no catfish or shrimp, meat and dairy cannot be prepared together, etc. Paul had been set free from these *"shadows,"* and now followed Jesus instructions in Mark 7:19, *"In saying this, Jesus declared all foods 'clean'."* But he did not allow his freedom to cause real trouble for others who were still weak in faith. When writing about meat offered to idols Paul wrote-

> "…food does not bring us near to God; we are no worse if we do not eat, and no better if we do. Be careful, however, that the <u>exercise of your freedom</u> does not become a stumbling block to the weak." (1 Cor. 8:8-10)

> "For I am not seeking my own good but the good of many, so <u>that they may be saved</u>." (1 Cor. 10:33)

> "IN ESSENTIALS, UNITY.
> IN NONESSENTIALS, LIBERTY.
> IN ALL THINGS, LOVE."

This is one of the mottos handed down from the Great Reformation that will help us understand Paul's motive for the things he fought for, and the things he chose to ignore. When he ate meat, and when he didn't.

Love, for the lost and for new believers, is the reason Paul said-

> "...to win as many as possible...so that by all possible means I might save some. I do all this for the sake of the gospel..."
> (1 Cor. 9:19-23)

Different Challenges In Different Cultures-

This also explains why Paul gave instructions about certain behaviors for churches in some countries, but not in others. There are specific reasons Paul gave these restrictions about women to the churches in the areas of Corinth and Ephesus, but not in Galatia or Thessalonica.

It should not be difficult for us to understand these localized instructions since we often follow the same patterns in evangelism today. Wise missionaries learn the local customs so that they do not unnecessarily offend people and make it more difficult to share the Gospel. Young people going on short term missions trips are usually taught how to dress, how to eat and how to speak while in a foreign country so they don't hinder the Message.

At my age, what remains of my life is all about leaving a legacy for my children and my children's children, and international leaders and the young leaders they are training. To accomplish this, I spend much of my time mentoring young men and women around the world. In doing this, I have learned that local customs and culture can help or hurt.

Could I Have Been More Offensive?

I learned on one of my first trips to Southeast Asia that one of my lifelong casual habits was deeply offensive to many Asians. Over the years, I would frequently cross my leg making the bottom of my shoe visible to others in the room. Or I would put my foot on an empty chair as I taught in order to keep the atmosphere causal and be approachable to my audience. During one teaching session in Malaysia, I casually put my foot on an empty chair and leaned forward to make a point. As I did, the temperature in the room seemed to drop by several degrees and I knew I had done something wrong. But I didn't know what it was.

As soon as the session was over, I asked my missionary friend what happened. I was told the bottom of shoes were considered, and rightfully so, to be the dirtiest part of the body, so it was very offensive for me to put my foot on the chair in front of these leaders.

This is why most Asians show respect by removing their shoes when they enter someone's home. I was also told to stop pointing with my index finger *(use my thumb instead)* because of the negative connotation it communicated to people in some parts of Asia and Africa. We remove our shoes here in Alaska, also. But it's so we don't track all the snow into the house.

Traditions like these are meaningless to the culture of the people where I grew up. Of course, we had different behaviors that would be just as meaningless or hard to understand in other cultures. But why not make concessions if it will help me communicate the Message more effectively? This was the same thought process Paul used when giving his temporary, cultural instructions to different churches in different places. Love will gladly give up its' personal liberties if it advances the cause of Christ's Kingdom!

Love will gladly give up its personal liberties to advance the cause of Christ's Kingdom!

Chapter Fifteen

The Challenge Of Our Own Bias

On our journey to understand why women's roles in teaching and church leadership seems to be so confusing, we have talked much about simplicity. We have established that in order to read the New Testament letters the way the writers intended them to be read, we have to follow three basic rules. We must discipline ourselves to-

(1) Consider the verses in context of the surrounding verses.
(2) Comprehend first century culture as it defines the words used.
(3) Compare Scripture with other Scripture about the same topic.

These three elements are simple, not always easy, but they don't have to be complicated. However, if we don't follow them, we will always read Scripture through the twisted lens of our culture. Our experiences, our prejudice, and our personal bias will guarantee we won't understand Scripture the way it was intended...until revelation comes.

As long as we read Scripture through our bias, we will make the same mistake the early church made. The simple truth is that their Jewish prejudice caused them to disobey their Lord. They didn't realize it but it's true. And we face the same problem each time we read the Word.

> **OUR PERSONAL BIAS WILL GUARANTEE WE WON'T UNDERSTAND THE SCRIPTURE THE WAY IT WAS INTENDED...UNTIL REVELATION COMES!**

How Racism Hindered the Great Commission—

For the first several years after Pentecost, the spread of the Gospel was greatly hindered by the deeply ingrained racism among many Jewish leaders. Jesus' original men refused to obey His final command.

I have found great resistance and unbelief when making this statement while teaching leaders around the world. None of us would want to believe that these great early leaders, most of whom became martyrs, blatantly refused to obey what we call Jesus' Great Commission. I'm sure they didn't realize they were rejecting His command. They didn't deliberately disobey. However, that is exactly what happened. And a simple reading of the book of Acts, while comparing Luke's account with a historical timeline, clearly shows that the early apostles heard Jesus' words in the Great Commission through racially biased ears, and just wouldn't do it.

Jesus had made it clear that as soon as the Spirit came upon them in Jerusalem, they were to GO, to everyone!

> **I'M SURE THEY DIDN'T REALIZE IT, BUT THEY DIRECTLY DISOBEYED BECAUSE OF RACISM.**

> *"Then Jesus came to them and said, "All authority in heaven and on earth has been given to me. Therefore go and make disciples of **all nations**."* (Matt. 28:18-19)

> *"You will receive power when the Holy Spirit comes on you; and you will be my witnesses in Jerusalem, and in all Judea and **Samaria**, and to the **ends of the earth**."* (Acts 1:8)

Jesus didn't seem to be complicated or cryptic at all.
> *"...go and make disciples of <u>all nations</u>."*
> *"...you will be my witnesses...to the <u>ends of the earth</u>."*

These words seem to be so simple, so clear, so easily understood. *"Wait for the Spirit, then Go to ALL nations...to the ends of the earth!"*

It seems so obvious that Jesus intended them to take the Good News to every country, every race, every tribe, and every genetic variation of human beings. It seems so clear that He wanted them to fulfill the promise made to their father, Abraham, "*I will make you a blessing to all nations!*" (Gen. 18:18) But they didn't believe that's what He meant at all!

They Did Not Actually "Go," They Were PUSHED!-
(These dates may not be exact but are based on best evidence available)

A simple, honest reading of the book of Acts shows that they didn't believe Jesus meant for them to go anywhere. So, they didn't go anywhere for years after Pentecost. And they didn't go then until the persecution got so bad, <u>they went to save their lives</u>.

> "On that day a great persecution broke out against the church at Jerusalem, and <u>all except the apostles were scattered</u> throughout <u>Judea</u> and <u>Samaria.</u>" (Acts 8:1-2)

FIVE YEARS After Pentecost!

The first places Jesus told them to go to after Pentecost were Judea and Samaria. They simply wouldn't go until <u>five</u> (5!) years after Pentecost. And they didn't go then out of *"joy to share the Good News,"* they went to escape persecution. They didn't really go; they were pushed!

TEN YEARS After Pentecost!

Jesus told them to take the Good News to all types of people. But no one shared the Gospel with any Gentiles until Peter was *"forced"* to go in Acts 10; this was <u>ten</u> (10!) years after Pentecost! And he didn't go to the

Gentiles joyfully. He had a strong rebuke in a vision that appeared to him three (3!) times before he was willing to go. And he was still afraid he was doing the wrong thing. Only after three visions and the appearance of an angel, was Peter willing to say, *"I now realize how true it is that God does not show favoritism..."* (Acts 10:34) Remember, this is a man who, for over three years, watched how Jesus lovingly welcomed sinners, Samaritans, Gentiles, and...women!

Only after the Holy Spirit filled this group of Gentiles, and Peter heard them *"speaking in tongues,"* was he willing to baptize them in water. And he was strongly criticized for doing such a thing!

> *"So when Peter went up to Jerusalem, the circumcised believers criticized him and said, 'You went into the house of uncircumcised men and ate with them'."* (Acts 11:2-3)

Read the story for yourself- Acts 10:1-11:18. It is full of insight about how our own prejudice can blind us to the most obvious truths. Truths about such things as women in leadership!

THIRTEEN YEARS After Pentecost!

And the first Gentile church was not founded in Antioch until thirteen (13!) years after Pentecost. And when it happened, the apostles didn't believe it! Many still refused to share the Good News with Gentiles!

> *"Now those who had been scattered by the persecution in connection with Stephen traveled as far as Phoenicia, Cyprus and Antioch,* **telling the message only to Jews.** *20 Some of them, however, men from Cyprus and Cyrene, went to Antioch and began to speak to Greeks also, telling them the good news about the Lord Jesus. 21 The Lord's hand was with them, and a great number of people believed and turned to the Lord."*
> (Acts 11:19-21)

Finally, ***thirteen years after Pentecost***, the Jewish believers begin to share the Gospel with Gentiles, at least in one Asian city. However, the internal fight among the apostolic leaders continued to grow, becoming more and more divisive.

TWENTY YEARS AND THEY STILL DIDN'T UNDERSTAND!

It is now ***twenty years after Pentecost*** *(20 YEARS!)* and many Jewish apostolic leaders were still adamant that Gentiles could not be righteous before God without fully converting to Judaism. Other Jewish apostles saw the fulfillment of God's original covenant with Abraham, not as an issue of having the genetics of Abraham or the Law of Moses, but having the faith of Abraham. They understood by this kind of faith, and by this faith alone, both Jew and Gentile could be made righteous, and made into ONE people of God. The disagreement continued to grow until it finally boiled over at the apostolic meeting in Jerusalem ***twenty years after Pentecost!***

> **The racism against Gentiles in the early church hindered the Great Commission for over *20 years* after Pentecost!**

-The Great Jew/Gentile Shootout in Jerusalem-

Acts 15 tells the story. After lengthy, heated arguments between the apostles about what Gentiles must do to be right with God, the leaders agreed to circulate a letter containing four simple commands. James, viewed as the senior leader, articulated their decision.

> *"It is my judgment, therefore, that we should not make it difficult for the Gentiles who are turning to God. 20 Instead we should write to them, telling them to abstain from food polluted by idols, from sexual immorality, from the meat of strangled animals and from blood."* (Acts 15:19-20)

> *"It seemed good to the Holy Spirit and to us not to burden you…"*
> (Acts 15:28)

The gathered leaders drafted a letter containing these four commands and ordered them to be circulated, by leaders who could read and answer their questions, to all the churches. Apostolic teams took the letter as they went to the churches throughout the Empire.

Paul agreed to these four *"commands"* in order to make peace among the apostles. But as time went by, sexual immorality was the only one he taught as being clearly wrong for all believers, in all cultures, while he viewed the others as non-essentials. He taught that meat offered to idols should be a matter of personal conviction and, out of love, was to be avoided if it caused those who are weak in faith to struggle.

> **Paul agreed to 4 commands but only taught one be to truly important.**

Animals strangled and things concerning blood were important in the Old Covenant. Even twenty years after Pentecost and all the talk among the apostles, some of the Jewish leaders still couldn't let go of some of the *"shadows"* in the Old Covenant that actually found their fulfillment in the shedding of Christ's blood. Knowing they were not essential for salvation and righteousness, Paul did not object. But he never taught them as having any merit. Paul explained his reasoning about the cultural aspect of the three nonessential *"commands"* to the Corinthian believers.

> *"So now, what about it? Should we eat meat that has been sacrificed to idols? Well, we all know that an idol is not really a god and that there is only one God and no other…7* <u>However, not all Christians realize this</u>. *Some are accustomed to thinking of idols as being real, so when they eat food that has been offered to idols, they think of it as the worship of real gods, and their weak*

consciences are violated. 8 It's true that we can't win God's approval by what we eat. We don't miss out on anything if we don't eat it, and we don't gain anything if we do. 9 <u>But you must be careful with this freedom of yours</u>. Do not cause a brother or sister with a weaker conscience to stumble."

(1 Cor. 8:4-9 NLT)

Once again, we see Paul willing to make concessions over nonessential things and giving up personal liberty in Christ for the good of younger, weaker believers.

> "...HE WHO LOVES HIS NEIGHBOR HAS FULFILLED THE LAW.
>
> LOVE DOES NO WRONG TO A NEIGHBOR; THEREFORE LOVE IS THE FULFILLMENT OF THE LAW."
>
> ROM. 13:8-10 NASB

<u>This will all be important as we look for answers to the final questions-</u>

**What did Paul really say about women?
Who did he say it to?
Why did he say it?
How do we apply his words today?**

Chapter Sixteen
What Did Paul Really Say About Women?

We have examined a large list of ways women have been honored in Scripture that don't <u>seem</u> to line up with the isolated instructions we have been told Paul wrote in 1 Corinthians and 1 Timothy. From the way Jesus ignored male-made rules in order to elevate women back to their original place of honor, to the way Paul honored women leaders just as he honored men, we see the behavior of the early church consistently saying, *"In Christ, there is neither male nor female."*

Finally, we have the clear biblical evidence that women functioned in virtually every leadership position possible in the early church, including the teaching of men. So how do we reconcile the confusing instructions in 1 Corinthians and 1 Timothy?

We have learned from looking at the world around us that when something seems to violate an absolute law, then we know that either <u>we don't understand everything yet,</u> or **there is more to the story**. Either way, we know we have to keep on searching to find the truth. And we know the search will be worth it because, once again, *"the truth will set us free."*

> **WE DON'T UNDERSTAND EVERYTHING YET... THERE MUST BE MORE TO THIS STORY!**

Certainly, the few passages in question are challenging to us in the 21st century because of the vast differences in language, culture, and chauvinistic influences over the past nearly two millennia. But these two passages seem to be in direct opposition to the model set by Paul and the early church. Sooo...there must be more to this story!

Remember, many of history's most influential men, from Aristotle (384 BC) in the *"secular"* realm, to Jerome (345 AD) in the *"Christian"* realm, have sadly reinforced the twisted view that there is something genetically inferior within women, all women. Their conclusion was that inferior genetics make women inherently second-class and not to be trusted. And this thinking has twisted the way many read and translate Scripture for far too long.

Let's remind ourselves that differing views of how women should function within the Body of Christ are very important for the fulfilling of everyone's calling; but not essential for salvation. We can disagree and still walk as brothers and sisters in Christ. However, I firmly believe this issue is so important that we must be diligent to make sure we get it right. Anything that disempowers well over half of God's people (women) is important; really important!

> **Anything that disempowers well over half of God's people is important; really important!**

Let's Get Technical, Simply Technical-

In order to fully appreciate why Paul wrote what he actually wrote, we have to get a bit technical about the context, culture, and language. To get to the technical heart of the issue, we also have to stay true to our belief in simplicity. To do that, we will examine these basic issues.

- *What are the words Paul actually wrote?*
- *What was the context in which he wrote them?*
- *How did Paul deal with the nearly universal problem of most women not allowed even the most elementary education?*

- How did the pervasive problem of goddess worship influence Paul's instructions?

Did Paul Really Say, "Silence, Ladies, Don't Say A Word?"

1 Timothy 2, when Paul used the word which many translators render, "*silent,*" we are given more evidence of the influence of male chauvinism on past Bible translations. And you don't have to be a language expert to see the gross inconsistencies.

The Greek word Paul used is "*hesuchia.*" In its various forms, the Greek word, **hesuchia**, means "*stillness, tranquil, undisturbing, live peaceful, keeping one's seat.*"

Paul uses a form of the word **hesuchia** 3 times in **1 Timothy 2**. And yet, in nearly every translation, **hesuchia** is translated differently when referring to people in general, and referring specifically to women.

> **1 Timothy 2:1-2-** "*I exhort therefore, that, first of all, supplications, prayers, intercessions, and giving of thanks, be made for all men; 2 For kings, and for all that are in authority; that we may lead a **quiet** and **peaceable** life...*" KJV

Here the word, **hesuchia,** is translated "***peaceable***." But just a few lines later, when referring to women, **hesuchia** is used twice, but translated very differently.

> **1 Timothy 2:11-12-** "*Let the woman learn in **silence** with all subjection. 12 But I suffer not a woman to teach, nor to usurp authority over the man, but to be in **silence**.*" KJV

Here the word, **hesuchia,** is *NOT* translated in any form of "***peaceable***." Strangely, it has been translated "***silence***" both times.

Looking back at 1 **Timothy 2:2**- *"...that we may lead a **quiet** and **peaceable** life..."* would any reasonable person think Paul was telling them to pray so they can live their lives in **silence**? I don't think so.

It seems odd, and sad, that when referring to people in general, **hesuchia** is translated "**peaceable**." But when referring to women just a few verses later it gets translated "**silence**," as in *"**don't say a word**."*

In all my study, and from searching out scholars far more brilliant than myself, I cannot give you a good reason why many translations are so inconsistent on this one subject, except blatant sexism. Minus the apparent male superiority, there would seem to be a simple and logical way to use language that we all would understand; the way we all use words in every day conversation.

"I Have A Peaceful Family And Live In A Quiet Neighborhood."

Our family has always been very vocal, pretty loud, and big celebrators. When we get together, we have a great time, we get all the fun we can out of everything, and it's always a challenge for the few quiet members of the family to get a word in, somehow. You would not use the Greek word, **hesuchia**, to describe our family get-togethers. We rarely act "hesuchia: *stillness, undisturbing, living peaceable, keeping one's seat."*

But many families seem to fully enjoy themselves while keeping the decibels down, the volume low. These families would be described as being *"gentle, quiet, and easy-going."* These families would be appropriately described as "hesuchia: *stillness, undisturbing, living peaceable, keeping one's seat."* But you would not say, *"They are completely silent, they never say a word."* That just wouldn't make any sense.

You may live in a *"quiet neighborhood."* But no one would take that to mean the neighbors *"never say a word,"* or *"remain completely silent."* It just wouldn't make any sense. We all know what <u>peaceful</u> means. My family may have a challenge in practicing *peacefulness*, but at least, we know what the word means.

Consider The Context of 1 Corinthians 11-14-

The context of Paul's writing about women's conduct in church meetings is included in his larger teaching on how <u>everyone</u> should conduct themselves as the Spirit moves in and through them in a public gathering. He writes about how to operate in spiritual gifts, especially vocal gifts, so that we help and not hinder.

> **How to operate in spiritual gifts so that we help and not hinder.**

He instructs them on how to control themselves with tongues and prophecy when it comes time for teaching; to not interrupt others, and to submit to the judgment of the group for the merit of what's being said. He sums it all up in this one instruction.

> *"For God is not a God of disorder but of peace, as in all the meetings of God's holy people."* (<u>1 Cor. 14:33 NLT</u>)

Remember, Paul is writing to people who met in houses in relatively small groups. This cannot be directly applied to our modern meetings without making adjustments for the larger numbers of people. In <u>1 Corinthians 14:26-40</u>, he gives his instruction in this context and order-

<u>When you come together for a meeting of the house church:</u>

- *Everyone should have something edifying to say.*
- *Be mindful that everything be done so all can understand.*
- *All can prophesy so that everyone may be instructed.*
- *When someone gives prophecy or revelation, the others should judge the merit of what is being said.*

- *You can control how the Spirit is working through you, so please do.*
- *God wants peaceful order so all will benefit.*
- *Women should not cause distraction and ask their questions at home.*
- *I want you all to be eager to prophesy and speak in tongues.*

<u>Paul ends by restating his most important guideline.</u>

"But everything should be done in a fitting and orderly way."
(<u>1 Cor. 14:40</u>)

Unless we are dealing with clear immorality and sin, what is *"fitting and orderly"* is always based on the culture in which you participate. We should know this based on Paul saying, *"I have become all things to all men so that by all possible means I might save some.<u> I do all this for the sake of the gospel</u>..."* (<u>1 Cor. 9:22-23</u>)

Chapter Seventeen

One Side Of The Conversation

One of the difficulties we face with several passages in 1 Corinthians is that we are only hearing one side of an important conversation. We are told that Paul is responding to a letter sent to him from Chloe and the house church she led. Earlier, in <u>1 Cor. 7:1</u>, Paul wrote, *"Now for the matters you wrote about..."*

Our challenge is that reading 1 Corinthians 7-15 is like overhearing only one half of a phone conversation. We have no way of knowing exactly what the Corinthians asked Paul. But, using a bit of logic and comparing other things Paul wrote, we can make an educated guess based on his responses.

<u>Let's Examine A Widely Accepted Scholarly Explanation-</u>
(*Keeping it simple, of course*)

First-century Greek doesn't have quotation marks as modern English does. But it does contain some accents and grammatical marks *(called "grave accents")* that help make it clear when the writer is quoting someone else. Those *"grave accents"* are present at the end of *"for it is disgraceful for a woman to speak in the church."* (1 Cor. 14:35)

This is why so many scholars believe this statement is NOT what Paul believed. Rather, he was quoting from the letter brought to him from Chloe and the church in her home. It does appear that some men in

Corinth were saying these things, claiming they represented Paul's position.

> "As in all the congregations of the saints, 34 women should remain silent in the churches. They are not allowed to speak, but must be in submission, as the Law says. 35 If they want to inquire about something, they should ask their own husbands at home; for it is disgraceful for a woman to speak in the church."
> (1 Cor. 14:33-35)

Certainly, there are things about the first century we will never know or fully understand. But we do know that Paul would not agree with this wooden literal translation because of all the ways he honored women who led and taught men; from Priscila, to Phoebe, Chloe, Junia, Euodia, Syntyche, Tryphena, Tryphosa, Persis, and many others.

If these incorrect statements about women were being made by men in Corinthian churches, and it resulted in wrong practices which Paul wanted to correct, that helps us understand the very next verse.

> "Did the word of God originate with you? Or are you the only people it has reached? 37 If anybody thinks he is a prophet or spiritually gifted, let him acknowledge that what I am writing to you is the Lord's command. 38 If he ignores this, he himself will be ignored."
> (1 Cor. 14:36-38)

<u>This is pretty harsh language.</u>

Paul was clearly rebuking some in Corinth for arrogantly believing their view was the only one that mattered. Especially wrong views that would shut down a majority of the converts, women, from allowing the Spirit to minister through them. Paul was the founder and overseer of most of the churches in Asia so he would certainly know the fallacy of this statement; *"As in all the congregations of the saints..."* The truth is...this was simply not true. And if anyone should know what the customs were in all the other congregations it would be Paul.

To give us further evidence that some were making up their own rules, we read this apparent quote from the letter to Paul from the Corinth church, *"They are not allowed to speak, but must be in submission, **as the Law says**."* (1 Cor. 14:34)

> **The truth is... this was simply not true.**

*"**...as the Law says**."* Is this from the Law or chauvinistic rabbis?

Paul certainly knew that this statement, *"They are not allowed to speak...as the Law says,"* is not found anywhere in the Law of Moses. But we do know, from quotes which are documented in earlier chapters of this book, statements like this *are found* in first century rabbinical writings by extremely chauvinistic rabbis afraid of Greek culture.

It is important to note that when writing in Acts 15, about the basic laws the Jewish apostles felt the Gentile converts should follow, there is no mention of *"women keep silent...as the Law says."* Why not? Because the Law does not require their silence.

Paul's Meaning Is More Simple Than It Seems-

With a little logic, Paul's instructions are not really complicated, at all. Let's suppose you are having a dozen people in your home every week for bible study and one of their five year old children blurts out a question. No doubt you would be kind and gentle. You may even try to give the child an answer simple enough for a five year old to understand. But, you wouldn't want to do that all night and every week. If it continued to happen, it's logical to assume that you would lovingly encourage them to ask their parents at home. Of course, you may want

> **They will... but not yet**

to have something for the children that would benefit them until they have enough understanding to participate in the adult Bible study.

This would have nothing to do with their gender, but their inability to understand and participate. They will be allowed to fully participate; <u>*just not yet*</u>.

Sound familiar?

This is how I would paraphrase Paul:
> *"Have the women in Corinth, who are just beginning to participate, keep their questions for after the meeting. They need to calm down, keep their seats, and learn. I know that this is very new for them and they are very excited about their new freedoms. But, tell them to go slow and be patient as they learn. The day will come when they will be able to function the way many of the women in other churches function for the benefit of the whole Body. Just not yet."*

You may be asking a very reasonable question about now:
> *"Wait a minute; I don't see a Bible verse that says all that."*

You are right. But, we must NEVER take "**<u>a</u>** *Bible verse*" to establish any complete truth. Considering context, comprehending culture and comparing all the Scriptures dealing with the subject, I fully believe the above compilation, in common English, is accurate.

Understanding that most women (not all) were forbidden any education at all, never allowed to even ask questions outside of their home, and that they were never permitted to participate in what we would consider to be normal conversation with men outside of immediate family, Paul's instructions make sense. Especially in the context of the first century Roman Empire.

This is the very reason Paul wrote instructions that, if he were writing today, I think it would go something like this:

> "I want the women to control themselves in the meetings. Don't chatter among themselves, or keep asking questions until they are ready and able to participate. Just listen to the teaching and let them learn from their husbands at home so they can grow and become equipped to fully participate. And, remember ladies, when you lead out in prayer or prophesy, be sure to have your scarves on so no one visiting the meeting mistakes you for a temple prostitute fortuneteller."

Remember,

Never Take Just "A" Bible Verse But Compare Them All.

Technology Makes It Easy To Do

Chapter Eighteen

Usurping Authority, Eve's Sin, And Childbearing

Paul's instruction to Timothy about women teaching men, Eve's original sin, and women being *"saved through childbearing,"* can certainly appear to be extremely confusing. Logic tells us to start with what is certain, what we know for sure, and use that information to help us understand things which seem confusing.

We can be certain that Paul didn't completely prohibit ALL women from teaching ALL men. We can be certain of this because of all the references in the New Testament that clearly show the many women who led churches and taught the Word without regard to gender.

> **Start with what is certain, what we know for sure, and that will help us understand things which seem confusing.**

When attempting to understand what someone meant, we can look at their behavior. When we try to understand what Jesus meant by, *"Love one another,"* we look to see how He acted toward others, how He treated *"un-lovely people."* To understand what Paul meant, just look at how he treated women who led with honor and gratitude.

> **To understand what Paul meant, we must look at his behavior.**

Paul's concern about some women when writing to Timothy was simple. He did not want unequipped women to *"usurp,"* or *"willfully assert themselves"* into functions and positions they were not qualified to fill…yet.

We can be certain of this because of the word Paul used to connect *"teaching"* with *"authority"* in 1 Timothy 2:12. Here is one of the times the King James Version (KJV) actually gives the best understanding.

> *"I suffer not a woman to teach, **nor to usurp** authority over the man, but to be in silence."* (1 Tim 2:12 KJV)

We have already found that this use of the word *"silence"* is sadly wrong. But the words, *"nor to usurp,"* are very important. The scholarly works listed in the back of this book clearly, and simply, show that the words *"teaching"* and *"authority"* are connected by the words, *"nor to usurp."* This is a strong Greek word which means, *"to act of oneself, dominate, autonomous, to be your own government."* It is the opposite of *"submission,"* which is required of all teachers/leaders, regardless of gender. It may be better written like this: *(my paraphrase)*

> **Neither men nor women should *"willfully assert themselves"* and *"set themselves up"* as teachers.**

> *"Do not allow unqualified women to* willfully assert themselves *and* set themselves up *as teachers, but to learn quietly until they have been equipped and released to lead by teaching."*

We Use Language In The Same Way-

Let's suppose I say to my sixteen year old, who has been having some difficulty acting responsibly, *"Do not leave the house or take the car* without my permission." There is a part of this sentence which we automatically assume, even though it's not actually said: *"...without my permission."*

> *"...without my permission."*

My sixteen year old would NOT understand that sentence to mean they must NEVER, EVER leave the house, no matter what the circumstances. But they would automatically understand it to mean:

> *"Do not leave the house, (<u>without my permission</u>,) or drive the car, without my permission."*

<u>This fits exactly with Paul's statement to Timothy:</u> *(my paraphrase)*

> *"I do not want women to willfully assert (usurp) themselves as teachers nor to willfully assert (usurp) themselves as leaders of men."* (1 Tim 2:12)

We know for certain this cannot be an absolute prohibition against all women, under every circumstance. We can be sure of this because of the way Paul honored Priscilla, Phoebe, Chloe, Junia, and many, many others. The model clarifies the meaning of Paul's words.

THE MODEL CLARIFIES THE MEANING

Did Eve Cause Original Sin? Are Women Saved By Pregnancy?

These are very important questions because the next verses say:

> *"For Adam was formed first, then Eve. And Adam was not the one deceived; it was the woman who was deceived and became a sinner. But women will be saved through childbearing, if they continue in faith, love and holiness with propriety."*
> (1 Tim. 2:13-15)

If we are going to isolate two verses that <u>seem</u> to say, *"Women, keep silent,"* and *"Women can't teach men,"* then we MUST be consistent and say, *"Original sin came through Eve and women are saved, not by grace through faith, but by simply giving birth."* If we only read this one passage, in this one translation, we would have to say:

> **(1) Sin came into the world through Eve.**
> **(2) Women can saved by simply birthing children.**

But, can either of these things be true? **<u>No, they absolutely cannot!</u>**

And how can we be so certain they are not true?

<u>By simply *comparing other Scriptures that refer to the same topic*.</u>

(1) <u>Did Sin Enter The World Through Eve?</u>

No, and Paul makes the answer crystal clear in <u>Romans 5</u>. Yes, Eve was deceived, but Adam knew exactly what he was doing, and did it anyway.

> *"When <u>Adam sinned</u>, sin entered the world...<u>Adam's sin</u> brought death, so death spread to everyone, for everyone sinned...Now <u>Adam is a symbol</u>, a representation of Christ, who was yet to come...For the <u>sin of this one man, Adam</u>, brought death to many...For <u>Adam's sin</u> led to condemnation...For <u>the sin of this one man, Adam</u>, caused death to rule over many...Because <u>one person disobeyed God</u>, many became sinners. But because one other person obeyed God, many will be made righteous."*
> (<u>Rom 5:12-19</u> NLT)

Paul says, at least 6 times in 8 verses, that sin came into the world by Adam's willful sin. Yes, Eve was deceived. And based on the same biblical passage, Genesis 3, Adam was so weak he made no protest, asked for no discussion, offered no opposing view, and as far as we know, he didn't even say, *"Wait a minute."* How does that qualify only men for leadership?

> Eve was deceived. But Adam made no protest, asked for no discussion, offered no opposing view, he didn't even say, *"Wait a minute."*

(2) Are Women Saved By Birthing Children?

Nothing can be more important than this question because it deals with the eternal condition of all women. The mistaken idea gained from isolating this one statement, *"...women will be saved through childbearing..."* is terribly destructive and high heresy! How can we be so absolutely certain this is false? Because we know from all the other Scriptures that salvation comes through faith in Christ's sacrifice, alone!

"For it is by grace you have been saved, through faith..." (Eph. 2:8)
"Everyone who calls on the name of the Lord will be saved." (Acts 2:21)
"Believe in the Lord Jesus, and you will be saved..." (Acts 16:31)
"For it is with your heart that you believe and are justified, and it is with your mouth that you confess and are saved." (Rom 10:10)

Consequently, we are reminded that we must NEVER take just a verse or one passage and build our doctrine on that limited perspective. So what did Paul mean by his statements about Eve's and childbirth?

Translations which use more modern English, such as the Amplified Version and the Message, really help us here.

> *"Adam was made first, then Eve; woman was deceived first — our pioneer in sin! — with <u>Adam right on her heels</u>. On the other hand, <u>her childbearing brought about salvation, reversing Eve.</u>*

> But <u>this salvation only comes to those</u> who continue in faith, love, and holiness, gathering it all into maturity. You can depend on this." (<u>1 Tim 2:13-15</u> THE MESSAGE)

> "For Adam was first formed, then Eve. And it was not Adam who was deceived, but the woman who was deceived and deluded and fell into transgression. <u>Nevertheless [the sentence put upon women of pain in motherhood does not hinder their souls' salvation</u>, and] they will be saved [eternally] if they continue in faith and love and holiness with self-control, [saved indeed] through the Childbearing or <u>by the birth of the divine Child</u>."
> (<u>1 Timothy 2:13-15</u> AMPLIFIED TRANSLATION)

Based on all the relevant verses, we can be sure that Paul <u>never</u> wrote, *"Original sin came through Eve and women are saved by simply giving birth."* He did write that Eve was deceived and part of what she reaped from her sin was pain in childbirth. But, because she endured by faith in God's promise, the *"Seed,"* the Christ, the One who would put an end to the Curse, came into the world through childbirth.

Of this, we can be certain. If we take one passage, *"Women be silent,"* in a wooden, literal way, then we must also say, *"Women are saved by birthing children."* It would be very dishonest to treat these verses differently. But if we dig a little deeper the complicated becomes clear.

Paul made it very clear.
When we are in Christ, everything changes.
There can be no blame or credit based on gender.
Each is dependent on the other as the Body of Christ.

"_In the Lord, however,_ woman is not independent of man, nor is man independent of woman. For as _woman came from man_, so also _man is born of woman_. But everything comes from God."
(1 Cor. 11:11-13)

> "You are all sons of God through faith in Christ Jesus, for all of you who were baptized into Christ have clothed yourselves with Christ. There is neither Jew nor Greek, slave nor free, male nor female, _for you are all one in Christ Jesus_."
> **(Gal 3:26-29)**

Chapter Nineteen

The Culture of Goddess Worship

There were good reasons for the commands concerning women not teaching in some circumstances, wearing head coverings when they prayed and prophesied, not styling their hair in certain fashions, and dressing modestly.

Pagan Worship, Prostitution, and Prophecy-

Pagan worship took different forms throughout the Empire. But, a common thread among most of them was the combining of sexuality and fertility rites with witchcraft, fortune-telling or *"prophecy."* Many major cities had pagan temples staffed with male and female prostitutes who could be hired to engage in sex and then prophesy or tell the fortune of the *"worshipper."* This was especially true in Corinth and Ephesus. Short hair, shaved heads, braided hair, seductive and expensive clothing, gaudy jewelry, and heavy make-up were all ways that were used to *"advertise"* the services of both the temple prostitutes and *"ordinary"* prostitutes.

This was all completely legal, and a first century person would find it common and ordinary. This is a main reason that moral, dignified women in Jewish, Greek and Roman cultures, were careful about how they dressed when going outside the home.

Virtually all women, not just Christian women, wore a veil of some kind to cover their hair and face whenever they left their home. It was the only way to keep from being constantly harassed by men thinking they could purchase their *"sexual/spiritual services."* Add religious teaching and prophecy to the mix, and it would be fairly easy to mistake a godly, believing woman for a temple prostitute.

Without a proper historical understanding, there is just no way a 21st century American believer could understand these 1st century customs by just reading the Bible verses.

But this should not be a surprise to us.

> **Virtually all "dignified" women covered their hair and face around men who were not family members.**

William Shakespeare made hundreds of cultural references in his writings that we would have no way of understanding without the research scholars have done about 17th century European culture. (*What is a "codpiece," anyway? Or for that matter, what's a "bustle"?*)

Remember, the people that the first century believers were *"evangelizing"* would be invited to home meetings where they would see women prophesying, and in some cases we have referenced, women teaching. These *"seekers"* would be very familiar with the way pagan temple prostitutes dressed, styled their hair, and the *"ecstasy"* they exhibited when being used by a *"spirit."*

We know Paul taught that believers were free from meaningless cultural and religious restrictions. But he gave guidelines so that cultural issues would not hinder the Gospel. He also gave these guidelines to protect and honor the believing women, not to demean or subjugate them!

What Was Unique About Corinth and Ephesus?

This was a particularly important issue in Corinth and Ephesus because each city had a primary temple to the Greek goddess; Diana (also called Artemis by Romans.) The temple in Ephesus is listed as one of the Seven Wonders of the Ancient World and its foundations can still be seen today. Timothy was an apostle to many of the churches in Ephesus when Paul wrote him about women learning in quietness and not appointing themselves as teachers.

Female priestesses had power and influence over many people living in the first century.

The powerful influence of this culture of goddess worship is a main reason Paul felt it was critical that women in the churches in Ephesus and Corinth give special attention to customs that were unique to their locations. He certainly didn't want believing women who led out in prayer, prophesied, taught the Word and served in other visible ways, to be confused with the women who served as prostitutes in pagan worship. Again, it's difficult for us to relate because their culture was so different for ours.

This was the reason both Paul and Peter instructed believing women to be careful about how they dressed. There was certainly nothing inherently evil about braided hair, make-up, nice jewelry, or expensive clothing. But the culture in both areas put women who were spiritual, who taught the Word of God, who led out in prayer and prophesied, at risk of being viewed as part of the daily practice of prostitution and fortune telling that was such a common part of pagan worship.

Once again, without reading some first century history, it's impossible to understand why Paul wrote some of what he wrote. The Holy Spirit inspired the biblical writers to pen eternal truth in a way their intended readers would understand. Of course, God had us, and every other generation, in mind. Apparently, He expected us to put forth a bit of effort to truly understand the truth that spans all generations. In this age of high tech, all we need to know is just a computer click away.

But we will not truly understand without a bit of common sense; the same common sense we use in reading any other written material from different cultures and different periods of time. We know Paul was not thinking about a 21st century audience; or even a 2nd century audience. He was writing to friends in cities that had unique situations who sought to see Christ's Kingdom built.

It just isn't possible for the average 21st century western believer to fully understand how common and public this religious sexual activity was in first century cities where Greek and Roman goddesses were worshipped. Nor is it easy to comprehend the power and influence female priestesses had over people because of their open sexuality, combined with supposed demonic curses and *"fortune telling,"* or *"pagan prophecy."*

It was the combination of a very different culture, and the nearly complete lack of even the most basic education for many women, that caused Paul to write the words that have caused so much confusion today. Remember, this may be confusing to us, but it was not to them. The people to whom Paul wrote understood what was read to them because they understood their culture. If they were dropped into the 21st century, they would need to learn about our culture just as we are learning about theirs.

> First Century believers understood the apostles' writings. However, if they were suddenly dropped into the 21st century, they would need a lot of explanation to understand us.

Chapter Twenty

Temporary Problem, Permanent Solution

The Temporary Problem Was Simple-

The problem concerning the role of women for most of the churches in the first century was simple. Throughout known history, women in most countries were forbidden an education and never allowed to participate in public dialogue, including the typical question/answer method used by teachers throughout history. The idea of women becoming teachers outside of the home wasn't even imagined in many parts of the Empire.

The result? The overwhelming number of women in the first century simply had no ability to function as a student, let alone become a teacher. This explains why Paul would write, *"Don't allow them to teach"* and *"they should ask their questions at home."* Sadly, because of generations of horrible treatment, many first century women couldn't even ask reasonable questions.

> **Teaching and training uneducated people makes this just a temporary problem.**

This should not be difficult for us to understand. Pull a 30 year old man out of the jungles of Sumatra, put him in a class with twelve year olds, and he couldn't ask a reasonable question, either! Or put a five year old in an algebra class and they would be completely lost. But the problem is not with gender and doesn't have to be permanent. Teaching and training of uneducated people makes this just a temporary problem.

False Teachers Take Advantage Of The Unequipped-

We have further evidence of this problem of completely uneducated and ill-prepared women in Paul's reference to the false teachings that were being spread in places like Ephesus. False teachers were taking advantage of the most vulnerable members and seriously harming many house churches.

> *"Some have wandered away from these and turned to meaningless talk. They want to be teachers of the law, but they do not know what they are talking about or what they so confidently affirm."* (1 Tim. 1:6-7)
>
> *"They get into the habit of being idle and going about from <u>house to house</u>. And not only do they become idlers, but also gossips and busybodies, saying things they ought not to*
> (1 Tim. 5:13-14 NLT)
>
> *"They are the kind who <u>work their way into people's homes</u> and win the confidence of <u>vulnerable women</u> who are burdened with the guilt of sin and controlled by various desires. (<u>Such women are forever following new teachings, but they are never able to understand the truth.</u>)* (2 Tim. 3:6-8 NLT)

Of course, false teachers would take advantage of the most vulnerable members. But this was a temporary problem in some areas and could not have been absolute for every single believing woman. We can be certain of this because, as we have read again and again, many educated, well-equipped women were, in fact, teaching. Priscila, as we have seen, was teaching in both

> **Many educated, well-equipped women were, in fact, teaching.**

Ephesus and Corinth even as Paul wrote these letters; with his clear endorsement and blessing. (Acts 18:2, 19) And some of Paul's letters were delivered and explained by well-equipped women, such as Phoebe and the letter to the Roman believers. (Romans 16:1)

Obvious Example, Obvious Danger-

We don't have to search too hard to find obvious, easy-to-understand examples in our present world. The conditions many women face today in extreme Muslim countries are nearly identical to what most women faced in the first century.

In many places today, they are not allowed to attend school, drive a car, speak to men outside of their immediate family, listen to world news, vote, testify in court, or go outside their home unless all but their eyes are covered. Most of us would want to be able to change all these prohibitions and set these women free, right now. But without a wise plan, think about the dangers we, and they, would face.

Just imagine what would happen if we were able to stand up tomorrow in one of these fiercely restricted countries and say, *"From now on, females have all the benefits and rights men have. From this day forward, you women can do anything men can do."* The idea might sound great but the result would be chaos and danger!

"Men drive cars, so you women can start driving now."
Chaos, danger! They would need lessons first. It would be a real problem, but only a temporary problem.

"Men are accountants, so now you women can be accountants."
Chaos, danger! They would need years of education. It would be a real problem, but only a temporary problem.

"Men are doctors, so you women can now treat patients."
Chaos, danger! They need medical school, first. Actually, they would need elementary school first. It would be a real problem, but only a temporary problem.

What makes all these important changes a problem is not gender, but education, preparation, and equipping. Some things will take a few days of training, while other things will take many years, just as it does for males. Once again, this is not a problem of gender, but preparation.

-The Permanent Solution- *"Teach Them"*

Since the temporary problem was that the majority of believing women were totally untrained and completely ill-equipped to do any public speaking or teaching or even ask worthy questions, Paul's long-term, permanent solution is simple- **"*Let them learn*."**

> *"A woman must quietly receive instruction…"* (1 Tim. 2:11 NASB)
>
> *"Women should learn quietly and submissively."* (1 Tim. 2:11 NLT)
>
> *"…they should ask their husbands at home."* (1 Cor. 14:35 NLT)

Over time, women were taught by their husbands, leaders and other educated women. As a result, they gained the knowledge and ability to speak with truth and wisdom, fulfilling their destiny in being a functioning, contributing member of Christ's Body.

Not a Novice, Not Yet.   Not A Woman, Not Yet-

Paul's instruction concerning unlearned women was completely consistent with the instructions he gave Timothy about not allowing a novice (*new convert- 1 Tim.3:6*) to be appointed as a leader. Because of a lack of basic education and experience, they were not prepared; not yet. It was clearly not meant to be a permanent prohibition for any one individual because, with training and experience, one was no longer a novice and could now be considered for leadership.

> **Consider Context-**
> **Comprehend Culture-**
> **Compare Scriptures-**

The commonly understood, but unwritten words in Paul's instructions are the words, "*not yet.*" The same is true of his restrictions on women in Corinth and Ephesus. *"You can minister and lead in any way God has gifted you. But, for those not yet equipped, <u>you can, just not yet</u>."*

Consider Context, Comprehend Culture, Compare Scriptures-

We followed our three basic rules for understanding literature, any literature, but specifically God's Word. We have seen that the context of Paul's instructions to the Corinthian believers gave them great liberty, both men and women, to allow the Spirit to work through them and to teach His word.   And the context also shows that he gave them reasonable guidelines for teaching and equipping so both men and women could be used by the Spirit in a valuable and orderly way.

-Important, But Temporary Problem?
Most first century women were completely uneducated and totally unequipped.

-Long-term, Permanent Solution?
Teach them! Train them! Equip Them! And Set Them Free!

Chapter Twenty-One

Long Answers To Short Questions

My wife, Linda, has been listening to me teach, preach, and answer questions from people around the world for over 45 years. She likes to say, *"Mark gives the longest answers to the shortest questions possible."* I choose to take that as the compliment I am sure she intends it to be.

I have attempted to give you as much biblical proof as possible so you can be certain of what you believe and why you believe it. Clearly, I have done that by giving very long answers to short, but very important questions.

HERE ARE THE SHORT QUESTIONS WE HAVE ASKED–

-Did Paul teach that women were to be silent in church meetings?

-Did Paul teach that women were never allowed to teach men?

-Does the New Testament teach that there are leadership ministries reserved only for men and never for women?

-Does Eve's deception show that men were created by God to be superior to women and be their "covering"?

A SUMMARY FROM THE LONG ANSWERS WE HAVE LEARNED–

To understand the meaning and intent of the apostolic writers, we have to have a basic understanding of the culture in which they lived. First Century Roman Empire, the individual nations conquered by Rome and the Second Temple Jewish society, all played an important part in the way the early believers lived and related to the world around them.

1) The vast majority of women were literally the property of men, believed to be genetically inferior to men, and genetically unable to be educated.

2) The vast majority of women had no civil rights and were never allowed to function in male society outside the home.

3) The vast majority of women were never allowed an education of any kind, even the opportunity to ask the simplest of questions.

4) The culture of goddess worship affected every layer of society, with Corinth and Ephesus being epicenters for the worship of Diana. Many of the instructions Paul gave to the churches he oversaw were to lower the risk of confusion with the priestess/prostitute/fortunetellers used in pagan worship.

5) Pentecost was the fulfillment of God's promise that God considers *BOTH* men and women to be His servants. God wants to fill *BOTH* men and women with His Spirit. And God wants *BOTH* men and women to speak on His behalf.

6) We have ample evidence in Acts and the Epistles that godly, educated, and equipped women were gifted by the Holy Spirit and encouraged to function in virtually every area of ministry.

7) When we understand the culture of the first century and the challenges believing women faced, we see clearly that Paul was not contradictory in his instructions. Instead, we understand that, like Jesus, everything Paul taught was meant to honor and elevate women. In ways society never did, but God always intended.

8) We have learned that the only way human beings truly manifest the image of God is when we, both male and female, allow His Spirit to live in and through us, and work together.

9) The serious, but **temporary problem** the Church faced was a long, long history of uneducated and unequipped women.

10) The **permanent answer** was, and still is, to teach and equip them. And give them the dignity and honor they fully deserved.

Finally, the most critical qualities required of anyone who ministered in the name of the Lord had nothing to do with gender. They had everything to do with *humility of heart* and *submission of spirit*.

> "*Submit to one another out of reverence for Christ.*" (Eph. 5:21)

> "*...submit to such as these and to everyone who joins in the work, and labors at it.*" (1 Cor. 16:15-17)

> "*Be completely humble and gentle; be patient, bearing with one another in love.*" (Eph. 4:2-3)

> "*All of you, clothe yourselves with humility toward one another, because, 'God opposes the proud but gives grace to the humble'.*" (1 Peter 5:5)

None of these instructions have anything to do with gender!

> THE TWO REQUIREMENTS FOR
> ALL WHO SEEK TO MINISTER–
>
> 1) HUMILITY OF HEART
> AND
> 2) SUBMISSION OF SPIRIT
>
> ...WITHOUT REGARD
> TO GENDER!

Chapter Twenty-Two

Sincere, Important Questions

Few readers can fully comprehend everything William Shakespeare intended in his writings of 500 years ago and writing in English (*well, some kind of English*). It's not likely that you and I will completely understand all that Paul referred to over 2000 years ago. In an entirely different culture. In a *"dead language"* no longer used. But we are dealing with the Word of God so we can be certain that the Spirit of Truth will guide us into all the truth we need to know for life.

I could not possibly address every question ever asked about this subject, but I do want to attempt to touch on a few. Please send me other questions and I will be happy to respond at:

askMark@markdrake.org.

(I may not be able to give wonderfully clear answers but I will respond.)

-*If these are temporary, cultural issues that don't apply to my culture, why would God preserve them in His Word?*

> Because they all contain principles of truth and serve as examples for us no matter where or when we live. The Epistles were personal letters that include many instructions that do not apply to us now but do contain eternal truths. For example:
>
> *"When you come, bring the cloak that I left with Carpus at Troas, and my scrolls, especially the parchments."* (2 Tim 4:13)

We would not consider these instructions to be meant for us.

All the Old Testament prophets spoke about events that were current to the people they were prophesying to, but do not apply to us today. However, the eternal principles and truths apply to all generations. Just a little logic and we can find them.

-Why didn't Jesus have a woman as one of the twelve disciples?

We can only speculate that since He did include women in His closest friends in all except the Twelve, and He did break nearly every other male/female taboo that wasn't sin, stepping over this final line was just too much, too soon. It may have been for the same reason that Paul observed some Jewish rituals and left some cities just for the sake of temporary peace.

He, also, did not include any Samaritans or Gentiles among the Twelve. Yet, we know His eternal plan would be that there is *"no Jew or Gentile"* just as there is *"no male or female"* in Him.

-Aren't women more easily deceived than men?

Certainly not. Not when both have the same opportunities to be equipped and trained. Far more men are mentioned in the Bible for heretical teaching than women. The Bible clearly shows that deception is the human condition, not limited to one gender. History shows that *FAR* more error came through men.

-Wasn't Eve deceived in the Garden and caused the Fall?

Yes, Eve was deceived. But, based on the same biblical passage, Adam was so weak he made no protest, asked for no discussion, offered no opposing view, and as far as we know, he didn't even say, *"Wait a minute."* How does that qualify him for leadership? Romans 5 makes it clear that the Fall came through Adam's willful disobedience, not Eve's deception.

"...just as sin entered the world through one man..." (Rom. 5:12)

-What about the "husband of one wife"?

Polygamy was common throughout the Roman Empire and also in first century Israel, but only for men. Women were not allowed to practice polygamy so there would have been no need to include them in this prohibition.

-When a woman leads shouldn't we know if her husband agrees and that she is submitted to him?

Definitely. Just as we should be certain that when a man leads, he is loving his wife as Christ loves the Church, with gentleness, kindness, unselfish love and with true understanding of her needs. Just as we need the wife's testimony that the husband obeys Eph 5:21- *"Submit to one another out of reverence for Christ."* However, I have rarely heard those questions asked by other men when considering a man for church leadership. Most questions seem to be about his gifting, *"anointing,"* and benefit to the church.

-But don't women who lead in church run the risk of being "out of order" by exhibiting domination, pride, deception, sensuality, emotion over logic, or mercy over truth?

Of course, women leaders/teachers can fail in all those ways. Just as men can and do exhibit every type of leadership failure possible. But when they do, we don't blame their gender. We blame their lack of letting Christ live in and through them, strengthening them from within, and manifesting His fruit of humility and accountability. These challenges of character are *"human"* based, not *"gender"* based.

-Isn't the husband supposed to be the "priest" over the home?

Absolutely not! This is a tragic mixing of Old Testament ideas with New Covenant truth. The Old Testament priesthood was fulfilled by Christ as our High Priest. Because He lives in each believer, men and women, all believers are part of the *"royal priesthood,"* without any gender-privilege.

"You are a chosen people. You are royal priests, a holy nation, God's very own possession." (1 Peter 2:9)

Husbands are told to serve as *"head of household."* As such, husbands are accountable to be managers for the good of the whole family, sacrificing themselves for the good of each member. The most important job of the *"head"* is to use the brain to *"think,"* not just the mouth to hand out commands.

-Do women need a male "covering" in order to minister in the church meeting?

No! Women need the same thing men need in order to minister and lead; humility, a submissive attitude and the approval of the other leaders. The New Testament teaching about *"covering"* applies only to a literal cloth because of first century culture. There is no mystical teaching about *"spiritual coverings."* Humility and fruitfulness are what matters.

-Aren't women easily influenced by the "Spirit of Jezebel"?

There is no *"spirit of Jezebel"* mentioned anywhere in the Bible. Jezebel was an extremely ungodly leader in Israel's history. The only reference to Jezebel in the New Testament is in Revelation 2 where John uses her as a metaphor of ungodly leaders who were influencing the church to immorality. Historically, men are guilty of sexual immorality far more often than women. The modern flood of pornography clearly proves this fact.

-If some of these passages are not translated correctly, how can we trust the authenticity of the Bible?

Because virtually all difficulties can be cleared up by comparing translations and understanding the culture in which it was written. Certainly, there is no disagreement or contradiction over the truths essential for life, godliness and salvation. There is more historical/scientific evidence to prove the unequaled trustworthiness of Scripture than for any other ancient book ever written! For the very best information see *"Has God Spoken?"* by Hank Hanegraaff.

-Are you saying there are NO differences between male and female? No differences in gender?

Certainly not! The two different sets of chromosomes result in far more differences than I am able to comprehend. And I love those differences. However, broad generalities are rarely accurate and never help.
("ALL women are like this..." "ALL men are like this...")

-Isn't it true that women are the "weaker sex"?

No. It is true that men, who are generally physically stronger than women and were viewed as superior in their culture, are told to honor women *"as if"* they are weaker for their protection and dignity. Even prayer is related to a husband's attitude and honor toward his wife.

> *"Husbands, in the same way be considerate as you live with your wives, and treat them with respect as the weaker partner and as heirs with you of the gracious gift of life, so that nothing will hinder your prayers."*
>
> (1 Peter 3:7)

Remember, first century culture generally treated women as possessions; degrading, abusing, and taking advantage of them.

But in Christ's community, husbands are taught to nurture, cherish, and value wives as they would their own bodies. We certainly would not want to handicap our own bodies. Why would we allow well over half of Christ's Body to be paralyzed, disabled or handicapped?   (Eph.5:25-33)

-Are you saying that there are no biblical restrictions on what giftings, ministries and leadership roles that women should be allowed to function in?

That depends. But it depends on the same things it should depend on for men to be endorsed to function in the same gifting and ministry roles.

>Are they equipped for the work they do?
>Are they living in true humility?
>Are they transparent and accountable to the other leaders?
>Does the example of their daily lives honor Christ or degrade the testimony of the Gospel?
>Are they open to and regularly seeking correction for the purpose of growth in their lives?
>Do the other leaders testify to the fruitfulness in their function?

–FINAL THOUGHTS–

A Severely Crippled Body of Christ– There is no better way to disable a person than to paralyze over half their body. Our enemy has convinced many believers that well over half of the Body of Christ is paralyzed and unable to function in many of the most important ways.

No Gender Privilege– After years of research, I firmly believe the Bible teaches that no female should be automatically disqualified from serving in any ministry role simply because of gender.

Liberty in Non-Essentials- Paul allowed liberty in what he considered non-essentials of the faith. We should seek a clearer view of what is truly essential. Let us not seek to "*Americanize*" the Gospel, but allow the Holy Spirit to cause the Kingdom to grow within every unique kindred, tribe, tongue...and culture. We must honor the leadership in each local church and not divide over non-essentials.

Recommended Reading

Everything I have presented about Scripture, culture, and history can be easily confirmed in the following list of resources, among many others. We live in an age where most information is just a click away.

-**What Paul REALLY Said About Women-** John Temple Bristow
-**Discovering Biblical Equality-** Pierce, Groothuis, Fee and others
-**IVP Bible Background Commentary-** C. Keener
-**Social-Science Commentary on the Letters of Paul-** Malina and Pilch
-**Social-Science Commentary on the Synoptic Gospels-** Malina and Rohrbaugh
-**Women in Ministry-** Jim Cobrae
-**10 Lies the Church Tells Women-** J. Lee Grady
-**Fashioned to Reign-** Kris Valloton
-**The Christian Women Set Free-** Gene Edwards
-**Why Not Women?-** Loren Cunningham
-**Two Views on Women In Ministry-** Belleville, Blomberg, Keener, Schreiner
-**How To Read The Bible For All Its Worth-** Gordon Fee

The simple guidelines I have tried to follow as we have examined the Scripture on this controversial subject are the same guidelines we must learn to use every time we read the Bible. That is the reason for this ever-growing series:

SIMPLE BIBLE / SIMPLE GRACE / SIMPLE ANSWERS

I would be happy to respond to any biblical questions you may have and you can help us build our world-wide library of answers to very important questions. Send your questions to **markdrake.org**.

-HELP US EQUIP LEADERS AROUND THE WORLD-

If you would like to help us get these materials freely to leaders who labor in the world's poorest places, join us as partners at **markdrake.org**.

> If you think women are the weaker sex, just try pulling the blankets back to your side of the bed. ☺

AUGUST 26, 1920.

Why is this date both a reason to celebrate and to grieve? **Celebrate** because women were finally given the right to vote. **Grieve** because it took thousands of years of nearly worldwide male dominance to overcome the belief that females were genetically inferior to males and not mentally fit to vote.

"It's a pickle jar, Tom... Twist the lid, not scripture."

Would you consider joining our team as a monthly partner?

Mark Drake International

Mark and Linda Drake

We can share in the fruit together as you help us train leaders and provide free resources in some of the world's poorest places where the Kingdom of God is exploding! From the jungles, to the barrios, to the slums, to the world's major cities; we are training leaders to train others with the message of true Grace and how to live in the New Covenant.

How We Handle Our Partner's Money-
Mark Drake International

-Everything you give goes directly into our mission.
-We live a modest lifestyle provided for by a small group of friends.
-We travel at the lowest cost reasonable.
-We give away as much as possible.
-We don't hire fund-raising companies.
-We don't purchase donor lists for solicitation.
-We do not use manipulation to prey on good people's compassion.
-We don't make unscriptural promises of quick riches if you give.
-MDI, Inc. is an IRS 501(c)3 non-profit, tax exempt organization.
-MDI has been given the highest charitable rating possible.
-MDI is accountable to a non-paid board of directors and home church.

-You can see what you will be a part of at markdrake.org.

IMPORTANT RESOURCES ABOUT LIVING IN THE TRUE NEW COVENANT

...plus much more at markdrake.org.

www.ingramcontent.com/pod-product-compliance
Lightning Source LLC
Chambersburg PA
CBHW070455100426
42743CB00010B/1630